Copy Cat

Written by Olivia George
Illustrated by Brett Hudson

My First READER

children's press ®

A Division of Scholastic Inc.
New York Toronto London Auckland Sydney
Mexico City New Delhi Hong Kong
Danbury, Connecticut

Library of Congress Cataloging-in-Publication Data

George, Olivia.
  Copy Cat / written by Olivia George ; illustrated by Brett Hudson.
      p. cm. — (My first reader)
  Summary: A kitten longs to be like the big cats until it finds something they can all do together.
  ISBN 0-516-24679-8 (lib. bdg.)   0-516-25113-9 (pbk.)
  [1. Cats—Fiction. 2. Stories in rhyme.] I. Hudson, Brett, ill. II. Title. III. Series.
  PZ8.3+
  [E]—dc22
                                2004000239

Note to Parents and Teachers

Once a reader can recognize and identify the 48 words used to tell this story, he or she will be able to successfully read the entire book. These 48 words are repeated throughout the story, so that young readers will be able to recognize the words easily and understand their meaning.

The 48 words used in this book are:

all	climb	get	lots	that
and	copy	go	me	the
are	day	grow	of	there
away	do	have	play	they
be	doing	hugs	purr	to
big	eat	I	room	want
call	everyone	is	say	what
can	for	it	small	you
cat	from	jump	so	
cats	fun	like	stretch	

Big cats have lots of fun all day.

They jump and purr.

They play and play.

I want to jump and play like that.

The big cats call me "Copy Cat."

The big cats climb. I want to go!

14

I want to eat so I can grow.

I want to stretch and purr all day.

They say, "Copy Cat, go away!"

What can small cats like me do?

Small cats can get hugs from you.

What are they doing? Can it be?

The big cats want to copy me!

Hugs from you are lots of fun.

There is room for everyone!

ABOUT THE AUTHOR

Olivia George was born and raised in Brooklyn, New York, and has spent her entire life surrounded by children's literature. She is, among other things, a childcare provider, a freelance editor and, of course, an author. Olivia has had many cats in her life, and one of her favorite activities is watching them play and interact with one another. She lives in Oakland, California, with her very own copy cat, Lola.

ABOUT THE ILLUSTRATOR

Brett Hudson graduated from Southampton University in 1997. Since then, he has illustrated many books for all age groups in addition to producing greeting cards and working on a medical magazine. In his spare time, Brett enjoys playing soccer and going to the movies. He and his partner, Lindsey, live near the sea in sunny Brighton, England.

Motorbooks International

MUSCLE CAR COLOR HISTORY

BARRACUDA & CHALLENGER

Paul Zazarine

First published in 1991 by Motorbooks International Publishers & Wholesalers, P O Box 2, 729 Prospect Avenue, Osceola, WI 54020 USA

Motorbooks International is a certified trademark, registered with the United States Patent Office

Motorbooks International books are also available at discounts in bulk quantity for industrial or sales-promotional use. For details write to Special Sales Manager at the Publisher's address

Library of Congress Cataloging-in-Publication Data
Zazarine, Paul.
    Barracuda & Challenger / Paul Zazarine.
        p.   cm.—(Motorbooks International muscle car color history)
    Includes index.
    ISBN 0-87938-538-3
    1. Barracuda automobile—History. 2. Challenger automobile—History. I. Title. II. Title: Barracuda and Challenger. III. Series.
TL215.B34Z39 1991
629.222—dc20   91-26808

Printed in Hong Kong

On the front cover: *The 1971 Plymouth 440 'Cuda convertible, here fitted with AAR 'Cuda side exhaust pipes added by the owner. Car courtesy of Rissler's Reproductions, Stevens, Pennsylvania. Mike Mueller*

On the back cover: *The 1970 Challenger T/A 340 was Dodge's homologation special for the Trans-Am series.*

On the frontispiece: *The name tag on the side of the Shaker hood scoop says it all: Hemi 'Cuda.*

On the title page: *A 1971 Challenger running in F/S manual lays down rubber during a drag race burnout.*

Contents

Acknowledgments

In the spring of 1963, stories began to leak out of Dearborn concerning a new sporty Ford to be called the Mustang. The rumours sparked a crash development program by the product planners at Chrysler to counter the car, which they thought would be nothing more than a dolled-up Falcon. Little did they—or anyone else in the car business in 1964—realize the success Iacocca's car would achieve. The Ford Mustang tapped a vein rich in sales, and the new "ponycar" market Ford mined would become one of the most lucrative of the 1960s.

Chrysler product planners chose to base their "personal sports car" on the Valiant platform, a sound economic decision since the only tooling necessary would be the fastback roof that designers had grafted to the Signet's C-pillars and deck. From a marketing standpoint, however, it wasn't nearly a large enough investment; the Barracuda failed to put a dent in the Mustang's sales. The 1964½ Mustang would outsell the 1964½ Barracuda almost six to one, and by 1966 Ford had eclipsed Plymouth, selling 1,288,557 Mustangs to 126,068 Barracudas. If Chrysler management had any visions on running neck and neck with Ford's sporty car, by 1966 it was obvious they were but pipedreams.

Instead of considering the early Barracudas a dismal failure, history has instead chosen to turn its back on the early years of Plymouth's sporty car, an indictment of Chrysler's sound economic yet poor marketing policy. Researching the 1964–1969 Barracudas was a challenge, because there aren't that many people who either know or care about the fastback fish from Highland Park. The main source of information on the early years came from Brandt Rosenbusch, the driving force behind the Chrysler Historical Collection and former owner of a 1967 Barracuda. His assistance and advice were invaluable in the assembly of information and photos from the Chrysler archives.

Equally as important to this book was Milt Antonick, who was involved in the design of all three (and the doomed fourth) generations of Barracuda and is the man who designed the original Barracuda emblem. The Design Studio photographs seen throughout the book are from Milt's private collection. Not only was he kind enough to supply copies, he also shared many memories and information never before published on the 1964–1974 Barracuda. My sincere thanks to him for his time and his help.

Antonick's colleague at the Dodge Design Studio, Carl Cameron, supplied details about his design work on the Challenger.

My thanks also to Dobbs Publications for permitting use of archival material from *Musclecar Review* and *Mopar Muscle* magazines, both of which I had the pleasure to edit in the mid- to late-eighties. Greg Rager, editor of *Mopar Muscle,* shared his recollections of being the first kid on his block to own a Barracuda and helped with technical information. *Musclecar Review* editor Tom Shaw provided much-appreciated assistance in finding shots of 'Cudas and Challengers.

My good friend Skip Norman at Gold Dust Classics (PO Box 6025, Ashland, VA 23005–6025) supplied the drag racing photography. Ron McQueeny and Bill Holder supplied the Challenger Pace Car photos. C. Van Tune, Tom Glatch and Dr. John Craft also supplied photos.

Thanks also to my editor at Motorbooks, Michael Dregni, who never ceases to inspire me with new ideas.

For a brief period in 1969, my father owned a Barracuda—a 1968 340 powered coupe. At the time I owned a 1966 383 Charger and was always trying to connive him into swapping cars for the day. I wasn't sophisticated enough to know why I appreciated the Barracuda's above-average cornering prowess. I just knew I liked the way it handled. It couldn't light up the rear tires like my Charger, but it was the first car I ever drove that was *fun* to take corners with. Thanks, Dad, for the keys to the 'Cuda.

Most importantly, this book is dedicated to my wife Nancy, who lovingly follows me on whatever path I have chosen to take through life.

Paul Zazarine

Introduction

Rise of the Ponycar

In the late 1950s, the profile of the American car buyer was undergoing a radical transition. The traditional customer had always wanted value, reliability and solid engineering, plus he savored the status of owning a new car. This buyer had weathered a depression and a world war, and once his pent-up thirst for new cars had been quenched, Detroit was forced to develop new reasons for buyers to feel the need to trade in and trade up.

A small percentage of those buyers, along with the emerging generation of new car customers born during World War II, were turning toward alternative transportation. Some of these buyers liked driving foreign-built vehicles, preferring the fuel economy and perceived quality in these foreign makes.

Because of these buyers, major European manufacturers like Volkswagen, Renault and Fiat registered sales gains in the American market. Some upscale buyers were moving toward Mercedes-Benz, while British sports cars like Triumph, MG and Austin-Healey were capturing a percentage of younger buyers. The combined annual sales of all these makes barely equaled the ten-day sales report of any division of the Big Three; however, it was enough to catch Detroit's attention. By the fall of 1959, the three major American car makers had fielded their versions of the "compact" car, designed to beat back the bulk of the foreign invasion.

Each of the three car makers had their own interpretation of what the small car

market demanded. Plymouth's Valiant (the Dodge Lancer would follow in 1961) had a sculptured, almost formal look with a six-window greenhouse and Imperial-inspired spare tire stamping on the decklid. Power was supplied by a six-cylinder engine. The Ford Falcon, a three-quarter-sized version of the big Ford, with traditional Ford styling cues like slab sides and large circular taillamps, was also powered by a small six-cylinder engine. And while GM would eventually field four compacts, the Chevrolet Corvair was the first into the breach and by far the most radical and most European-influenced of all the American compact cars. The Corvair was a rear-engine design utilizing a horizontally opposed six-cylinder air-cooled powerplant and independent rear suspension. Like its engineering, the Corvair's styling was unconventional and shared little with other Chevrolet products.

Initial sales were strong, with more than 250,000 1960 Corvairs sold. Ford's more conventional Falcon registered 435,676 units sold, while Plymouth rounded out the pack with sales of 194,292 Valiants.

In the following three model years, each car maker would take a different tack to increase market share and define the purpose of the model. As was often the case, to meet buyer demand the compacts began to change, offering more options, which boosted the low sticker price—originally one of the prime selling points for the smaller cars.

Car makers didn't like small cars because the profit margins were slim and generally small car buyers didn't add many options to fatten the sticker price and increase profits. To raise per-unit profits, car makers took advantage of the transition in buyer's tastes by adding accessories and hiking prices.

Shifting buyer demands also changed marketing techniques; by 1963, sales of the Ford Falcon were down 30 percent, and the other compacts weren't faring much better. Ford responded by adding a V-8 in 1963, and Plymouth installed a 273 ci V-8 in 1964. "Apparently," *Motor Trend* observed, "John Q. is off the '59-'61 economy kick."

It was Chevrolet's Corvair Monza, however, that launched the beginning of the phenomenon that would culminate in the Mustang and all the cars it would inspire. By 1962, more than 64 percent of all Corvairs were equipped with bucket seats and 38 percent had four-speed gearboxes. Also by 1962, the Corvair Monza Spyder was redefining the small American sporty car. The Spyder still retained the Corvair's rear-engine platform, however it had captured the interest of sports car enthusiasts, thanks in part to its European flair and a 150 hp turbocharged version of its air-cooled six-cylinder engine. By 1963, the Monza series was outselling the base Corvair almost seven to one, with sales of more than 204,000 units.

The Corvair's sales numbers weren't all that caught the eye of Ford's Lee Iacocca. He was more impressed with

A 1971 Challenger burns out on takeoff at the drag strip. The TorqueFlite automatic was a favorite among straight-line acceleration buffs as it was consistent in turning good times.

8

the buyers the Corvair Monza was attracting. These buyers were younger, better educated and also consisted of more single women than ever before. Iacocca saw the opportunity to bring to market a sporty car that would wrangle away those buyers, and he could build it on the Falcon platform, which allowed him to deliver the car cheaply and quickly. And he could offer something the Corvair couldn't: V–8 power.

The success of the Mustang overwhelmed the car industry. In the first four months after the Mustang's introduction on April 17, 1964, Ford sold more than 100,000 units. By the end of the 1966 model year, less than thirty months after it had been released, Ford had delivered more than 1.28 million Mustangs, shattering all-time industry sales records.

The ponycar market spawned by the Mustang was clearly defined by 1967 as other car makers fielded their versions. Plymouth had quietly slipped into the fray two weeks before the Mustang had been introduced with a fastback version of the Valiant. Yet the Mustang grabbed all the headlines, and Ford hurriedly added more manufacturing capacity to meet an unprecedented demand. Plymouth slowly crystallized the Barracuda's identity, and while it never equaled the Mustang's popularity, the Barracuda developed a following that ranged over the years from SCCA rally drivers to Trans-Am racers to drag racing's quarter-mile gear pounders.

To its credit, the Barracuda—and later its Dodge Challenger clone—retained Chrysler's unique engineering and styling. By 1970, the Barracuda was a far cry from the original Valiant platform that had been fielded to fight the foreign invasion. The 'Cuda, as it was now called, and the Challenger sported powerplants up to 440 ci and more than 425 hp. To compete in the dynamic automotive market, the Barracuda had made the transition from sporty car to musclecar.

Like other musclecars in the early 1970s, the Chrysler E-body twins were mortally wounded by a coalition of forces arrayed against high-performance automobiles. By levying premium surcharges against musclecars, the insurance industry had made it tougher for young drivers to own and maintain these cars. Compounding the problem were voices in and out of government critical of Detroit for selling the

The XY2, drawn by Dave Cummins in 1960, was his vision of a turbine-powered sports car for the future. While it retained some of Chrysler's design concepts from the 1950s, the XY2 also contained many styling cues that would eventually find their way into sketches and clays, and in some cases, production cars of the 1960s. Cummins would later translate the XY2's large rear glass area and semifastback into the Valiant Fastback and eventually, the 1964 Barracuda.

young drivers what were considered "lethal weapons." The final blow to musclecars was the shift in emphasis from performance to research as Detroit struggled to meet upcoming federal mandates for cleaner engine emissions.

By 1974, the Barracuda and Challenger were doomed as ponycar sales continued to plummet. And while proposals were made for a new generation of Barracudas and Challengers, Chrysler management was not interested in perpetuating a product line that didn't fit into its future plans. These plans were filled with mid-sized Aspens and Volares and compact Omnis and Horizons. There was no place for sporty high-performance cars.

And yet, one can't help but wonder what would have happened had Chrysler approved a new generation of E-bodies. Compared to GM's Firebird and Camaro, the clays of these doomed proposals were fresh and exciting. Could Chrysler's ponycars have carried the corporation through the drought of the mid and late 1970s? One can point to Pontiac, where the Grand Prix and Firebird accounted for the lion's share of sales and kept the division afloat from 1975-1980. Firebird sales alone climbed from a low of 29,951 units in 1973 to 211,484 units in 1979, accounting for almost two out of every five Pontiacs sold that year. This increase in sales was part of an upturn in the ponycar market that no one in Detroit anticipated. What makes the Firebird's sales performance more extraordinary is that Pontiac's marketing group had recommended killing the Firebird when it was on the ropes in the early 1970s in favor of smaller, more conservative cars. The decision to retain the Firebird played a major part in Pontiac's survival.

When the decade was over, the ponycar had survived, but two important nameplates—Barracuda and Challenger—were gone. If Chrysler had produced a new generation of E-bodies, the corporation's fate in the late 1970s might have been kinder. Chances are it would still have run aground; however, Chrysler's condition might not have been as tenuous. The Barracuda and the Challenger would not have saved Chrysler, but it's possible their sales could have softened the blows Chrysler suffered in the dark days of the late 1970s.

Inspired by Italian sports cars, the 1965 Barracuda's parking lamps were incorporated
into the grilles. Plymouth's sporty car was
almost named something else in 1964. In the
slang lexicon of the era, a "barracuda" was a
woman on the make or a prostitute. That fact
eluded management, and the fish went to
market.

Barracuda 1964–1966
Fastback Fish in Valiant Clothing

In the summer of 1962, a young designer named Milt Antonick walked into the Plymouth Design Studio for the first time. Antonick, who had been part of the Raymond Loewy team that designed the Avanti, had left Studebaker and signed on with Plymouth. Plans to reskin the Plymouth Valiant were already under way when Antonick arrived. Upon entering the studio, one of the first things to catch his eye was a nearly full-sized airbrush rendering of a modified Valiant sporting a new roof and grille. It was called the Valiant Fastback.

The concept of a fastback Plymouth was nothing new when designer Dave Cummins sketched his ideas for the Valiant. In 1959, long before Chevrolet used the name "Super Sport," Plymouth designers had conceived a long-deck mid-sized SS model with a fastback wraparound backlight. The Super Sport was a proposal for 1962 introduction, and went all the way to clay before being scrapped. Its unusual backlight intrigued Plymouth designers like Cummins, who eventually transferred it to the Valiant.

The word was already circulating that Ford was going to release a sporty car called Mustang and, as Antonick recalled, "because of that, the Valiant fastback got the nod." By late 1962, Plymouth designers had completed the final clays for the new fastback, which shared most of the Valiant's sheetmetal with the exception of the roof and the grilles.

At the time, bringing a new model to market usually took three to four years, so to get the Barracuda out in less than two years required compromises on both design and engineering. In fact, the design of the first Barracuda was restricted by the Valiant's engineering. "All of the cars had gone to unibody," Antonick recalled, "and for any program we never could do the amount of sheetmetal because it was tied into too much expenditure and the company wasn't that large. Tooling costs weren't proportionate to company size, they were proportionate to tools."

Another factor that anchored the new model to its Valiant heritage was Chrysler's view of the small car market. Like

Styling studio photograph taken April 12, 1963, shows the Barracuda's exterior was already close to completion. The dummy side-pipe was abandoned in favor of a smooth bright molding at the rocker panel. Aftermarket wheels were not considered for production models. "The flowing headlight look, a little bit of a wing effect, the bumper lower wing, with the hood acting as an upper wing connected in the middle by the grille," recalled Barracuda designer Milt Antonick, "were all Chrysler themes in the late fifties and early sixties." Note Valiant Signet emblems on fenders.

every other car maker, Chrysler made its money in big cars, which had always been the staple of the product line. Chrysler management was so conservative that the only modifications approved for the Barracuda was the roof and the grille, along with the inexpensive interior changes.

1964: Debut of the Fastback Fish

On April 1, 1964, just over two weeks before Ford introduced its Mustang, Plymouth unveiled the Barracuda. Although the Barracuda was unlike the Mustang's long hood and short-deck styling, it was unique enough to post sales of 23,443 units in the four months that remained in the 1964 model year.

Also, unlike the Mustang, which was offered in either coupe or convertible styles, the Barracuda was only available as a fastback. And it was a unique fastback, a claim substantiated in fact, since it possessed the largest single piece of window glass ever installed in a passenger car. The rounded fastback look was accomplished by angling the C-pillars back and pulling the decklid upward to meet the backglass at the beltline level.

If the fastback wasn't enough of an identifier, the Barracuda also received a distinctive front end with large circular parking lamps placed deep in the grille screens, single headlamps and a thin bar front bumper. Barracuda script was placed high at the rear of the front fenders near the door line. Around back, the Valiant nameplate appeared on the right rear of the deck. The rear quarters hinted at just the faintest trace of a tailfin with wide vertical taillamps atop round reverse lamps.

The Barracuda's interior was plush, with door-to-door carpeting and padded bucket seats. Door and quarter trim panels were embossed with a horizontal rib pattern that matched the seat upholstery. What made the Barracuda's interior especially unique was the versatility of the rear passenger and storage areas. The rear seat folded down to fit flush with the floor behind it, creating 23.7 sq–ft of usable luggage space. And, since the back side of the rear seat and

The original inspiration for the Barracuda's unusual backlight came from the Plymouth Super Sport. Drawn in 1959 by designer Tom Ferris, the Plymouth SS went all the way to clay before cancellation; it would have been introduced as a 1962 model. When Chevrolet released its SS in 1961, Plymouth shifted its designation for hot models to Formula S. That designation eventually found its way to the 1965 Barracuda.

Factory photos clearly illustrate the Valiant family heritage below the beltline. The backlight, supplied by PPG, was the largest single piece of glass installed in any American production automobile.

Whatizzit?
A Boy and His Fish

By Greg Rager

I was 17, in the Navy and naturally, somewhat cut off from mainstream America. Being a car nut made this an especially frustrating situation. Extended periods at sea of nine months or more were not conducive to keeping abreast of the new models, who was hot in racing and on the street, and with what car and equipment.

One bright side to it all was an eighteen-month shipyard period in 1964–1965 during which I was able to make it home nearly every weekend. With no car of my own at that point I looked forward to getting home, walking in the door, saying "Hi, mom," grabbing the keys off the table and heading for the garage and her '60 Imperial convertible. But this day something was different—the keys were not on the table as was customary. Mom explained she had left them in the car.

As I opened the garage door my mind suddenly went into a shock mode. The Imperial was gone. In its place was a brand new, sporty, little (compared to the Imperial), white fastback "Whatizzit". As I walked around the car, I took inventory of the features: Plymouth nameplate (OK, it's a Mopar. So far, so good), bucket seats and . . . what's a Barracuda? Oh yeah, it also said V–8 on the front fenders. The keys were in the ignition and my driver's license was in my wallet. It was time to ride.

Within a short distance I just had to stop and find out what made the thing tick. Under the hood I found a small V–8 totally unfamiliar to me. The owner's manual identified it as a 180 hp 273 two-barrel. It sure felt like more than that in the lightweight Barracuda.

After a few hours I began to get used to people staring and pointing. Although it was a bit awkward at first when people would ask "Whatizzit". I still wasn't exactly sure myself. There was the time, when sitting at a traffic light on Main Street, the girl in the crosswalk asked if it was a Sting Ray, and I of course answered, "No". Her reply was "Oh, I just love Sting Rays". It was too late to re-think my answer as she walked away. Mom later explained all she knew about the car and a trip to the dealership filled in the blanks. In any event, it was the first 1964 Barracuda sold in Johnstown, Pennsylvania.

Over a period of about a year that "Whatizzit" and I shared many a pleasurable moment. One of my favorite pastimes was driving down crowded Main Street in the middle of the day, with my crazy buddy Peppy in the back window doing his

continued on next page

A boy and his fish. Greg Rager and his mom's Barracuda.

continued

"goldfish in a bowl" act. The Barracuda was already especially noticeable as I was particularly fond of stopping a few blocks from home, jacking the front end up and putting 2x4s in the lower control arms to make it sit like the Ramchargers and other race cars of the era. Peppy's act just added to the impact.

As time passed I bought my own car, got discharged from Uncle Sam's Canoe Club and moved back home. Mom traded the '64 on a yellow '68 Barracuda notchback coupe. Occasionally I would spot the '64 around town. I could recognize it by the two Phillips-head screws in the rear panel where I had removed the pot-metal dealer name tag and used the screws to fill the holes.

One day, around 1980, I saw "Whatizzit" for the last time. It and about eight other cars were on a truck, each of them about a foot tall. They had just come from a date with the crusher and were en route to a local scrap metal yard. The three Phillips screws jumped out at me as if they were a neon sign. I followed the truck to the yard and watched as "Whatizzit" was dropped into a multi-car heap by a huge magnetic crane. My stomach turned into a knot as I said good bye to an old friend. I had courted my wife in that "Whatizzit".

the floor were also carpeted, as was a hinged "security panel" that could also be folded down, a large utility space was created, a full 7 ft. long from front seat back to rear bumper. With the security panel in the upright and locked position, the trunk offered 5.7 sq-ft of luggage space and could only be accessed by opening the decklid.

The instrument panel was simplistic in style and execution, with round pods containing the instrumentation surrounded by a bright bezel. Controls for headlamps and windshield wipers were to the left of the panel, while switches for the heater and defroster and the cigar lighter were to the right, situated in the center of the instrument panel, directly above the optional radio. The bright trim theme extended across the dash, terminating at the far right-hand

European influence was evident in the Barracuda's front grille and parking lamp treatment. The thin bar bumper and rounded valance panel continued the European styling.

The Barracuda gained instant recognition for its versatile fold-down rear seat and utility area. With the seat folded down and the trunk compartment opened, more than 7 ft. of carpeted cargo space was available.

end of the panel. The standard steering wheel was a two-spoke affair with a chrome horn ring. A plastic, wood-grained three-spoke steering wheel was optional.

The Barracuda buyer also had option choices to dress up his purchase. Power steering was offered, as were two-speed wipers with washer, day-night inside rearview mirror, air conditioning, reverse lamps, limited-slip differential and a driver's side remote control outside rearview mirror.

The standard Barracuda engine was a 170 ci Slant Six producing 101 hp at 4400

The 1964 instrument panel was simple and well laid out. This Barracuda is equipped with TorqueFlite automatic transmission, which in 1964 still used push buttons for gear selection. Beginning in 1965, the automatic selector would be located either on the column or in the console.

When equipped with four-speed manual transmission, a Hurst shifter was standard. Note the instrument panel pad and the misaligned glovebox door on this early prototype interior.

rpm and 155 lb-ft of torque at 2400 rpm. A 225 ci Slant Six rated at 145 hp at 4000 rpm was optional. This meatier version of the Slant Six cranked out 215 lb-ft of torque thanks to a longer 4.125 in. stroke. Top of the engine line was a 273 ci V-8 that produced 180 hp at 4200 rpm and 260 lb-ft of torque at 1600 rpm.

This 1965 pre-production photo actually showed a 1964 Barracuda, evidenced by the Valiant script next to the right taillamp and 1964 instrument panel as seen through the passenger door. The wide body stripe was offered in 1964 and carried over to 1965 for Formula S models.

Transmission choices began with a three-speed manual gearbox with the shifter mounted on the column. Stepping up to the larger six or V–8 engine allowed the buyer to add either a four-speed manual transmission with floor-mounted Hurst shifter or the three-speed TorqueFlite automatic transmission with dash-mounted push-button gear selector.

Under the sheetmetal, the suspension consisted of rear leaf springs and Hotchkiss drive. Up front, the Barracuda featured Chrysler's unique torsion-bar suspension. Drum brakes at all four corners utilized bonded linings. Mounted on 4.5 in. rims, the 6.50x13 tires were offered in blackwall or optional whitewall styling. There were two wheel cover options, a mag-style sport cover with exposed chrome-plated lug nuts or a ribbed cover with simulated knock offs.

1965: Building Muscle

For 1965, the Barracuda underwent little change. The emblems were revised with the Valiant nameplate removed from the rear deck. Inside, the instrument panel was redesigned, with two

pods on either side of the steering column containing the speedometer in the left pod and the fuel, temperature and ammeter gauges in the right-hand pod. A new option was a 6000 rpm tachometer installed in the lower left section of the dash next to the speedometer. On automatic transmission-equipped models, the push-button selector was replaced by a column-mounted shifter. A floor-mounted shifter in a small consolette located between the front seats was also offered for 1965.

The big news for 1965 was that the Barracuda had grown some muscle. Known as the Formula S Package, this new option was a superb balance of suspension and engine performance. Immediately recognizable by the racing stripe

17

Front of pre-production 1965 Barracuda. With the exception of minor changes to ornamentation and emblems, the exterior was unchanged from 1964.

Optional for 1965 (standard as part of the Formula S Package) was this 6000 rpm tachometer. Mounted at the far left end of the instrument panel next to the speedometer, it was difficult to see.

that ran right down the middle of the Barracuda and special model medallions on the front fenders, the Formula S started with a hot new version of the 273 V–8 called the Commando.

This engine was rated at 235 hp at 5200 rpm and produced 280 lb-ft of torque at 4000 rpm thanks to the addition of a Carter AFB four-barrel carburetor and domed, lightweight aluminum pistons with a 10.5:1 compression ratio. The high-lift, high-overlap camshaft featured 0.415 in. lift on intake and 0.425 in.

exhaust. Valve diameters were 1.78 in. for intake and 1.50 in. for exhaust, both using single springs. Also part of the Commando 273 package were dual breaker points, solid lifters and a low-restriction single exhaust with resonator and large rectangular tip. The Commando 273 was dressed up with valve covers finished in black crackle paint with aluminum fins and a chrome air cleaner topped with a Commando 273 plate. A 6000 rpm tachometer was also part of the package.

All of this engine hardware combined to give the Barracuda some impressive performance numbers. With 3.55:1 rear gears, the Commando 273 could propel the 3,150 lb. Barracuda from 0–60 mph in 8.5 sec. and through the quarter-mile in 16.5 sec. at a trap speed of 85 mph. Top speed was around 110 mph.

But straight-line acceleration wasn't really the Formula S Package's forte. The suspension received considerable attention, including heavy-duty front torsion bars, stiffer rear springs with additional leaves, Firm Ride shock absorbers and front antisway bar. Wheel width was increased to 5.5 in. and diameter to 14 in. And, while drum brakes were standard at all four corners, front disc brakes were offered as a dealer-installed option.

Working with Goodyear, Plymouth fitted the Formula S with a special version of the Blue Streak performance tire. Blue Streaks were standard fare on police packages and race cars, and the suggestion of high-performance complemented the Formula S Package. While the 6.95x14 Blue Streaks used on the Formula S were of a much harder compound and different tread design for passenger-car service applications, they did provide better adhesion. It was an excellent marketing move to have tires on the Formula S that enthusiasts automatically related to performance. A chromed wheel cover dressed up the package.

Once the basic package was checked off, the buyer could then add a variety of options, including power steering and brakes, four-speed manual gearbox with Hurst floor-mounted shifter, three-speed TorqueFlite automatic transmission on the column or on the floor in an optional consolette, reverse lamps, limited-slip differential, sport steering wheel, AM radio, seat belts and safety padding for the dashboard.

While Plymouth was still searching for the right image for the Barracuda, the Formula S Package was a step in the right direction. Not only did the Formula S perform well on the street, it also nailed down the 1965 SCCA rally championship. For the time being, Plymouth was betting the rent on the European-type

Chrysler engineer Scott Harvey used his expertise as a rally driver to select the high-performance suspension components used in the Barracuda Formula S. The package added stiffer springs and shocks, front anti-sway bar and Goodyear Blue Streak performance tires, and transformed the Barracuda into a balanced, well-handling sports car. Plymouth was proud enough of the Formula S to run a series of ads touting their new sporty car.

Previous page
The 1965 Barracuda in Ivory with gold stripe. Not all high-performance Barracudas were equipped with the Formula S Package. This

Barracuda has the Rally Pack which consisted of the Commando 273 engine and special suspension with heavy-duty springs and front anti-sway bar and heavy-duty shocks.

The Barracuda's interior was plush, with door-to-door carpeting and padded bucket seats upholstered in vinyl. Interior colors offered were gold, red, blue or black.

Drag Racing the Barracuda

Soon after it was released, the Barracuda began showing up on the dragstrip. By 1965, some versions, like the Golden Commando's *Goldfish,* used a highly modified 273 ci engine and competed in F/Stock, winning its class at the 1965 NHRA Nationals with a 13.47/103.68.

Another popular configuration was to drop in a super-charged 392 Hemi, install a narrowed rear axle and replace the torsion bars with a solid front axle. Bob Sullivan from Kansas City ran this set up in an all-steel-bodied 1965 B/Fuel Barracuda dragster named *Pandemonium.* Sullivan's best effort was a 10.21/151.48.

Perhaps one of the largest surprises of the season was Richard Petty and his 43/JR *Outlawed* Barracuda. Petty ended up drag racing when Chrysler boycotted NASCAR in 1965, and to compete he chose a Barracuda. The car was completely stripped and the rear wheelhouses were tubbed to accommo-date slicks. A 426 Hemi was installed and the firewall was moved rearward to allow room for the Elephant Engine, which placed the driver further back from the stock seating position. After a try at gas, Petty switched over to fuel and injected the Hemi to run in the funny car class. Petty usually clicked off the quarter-mile in the 10.14/136.98 range—not bad for a roundy-rounder! Unfortunately, a tragic accident that took the life of a young fan cut Petty's drag racing career short.

Several versions of the *Hemi Under Glass* were fielded. One of the first was the *Hemi-Cuda* sponsored by the Southern California Plymouth dealers and driven first by Tom McEwen and later Fred Goeske. In this car, a Hilborn-injected, blown 426 Hemi delivering 1000 hp on 80 percent nitro was placed directly in the middle of the car behind the driver's right shoulder. The first *Hemi-Cuda* went airborn at 150 mph on its fifth pass and was completely destroyed, although McEwen was uninjured.

The second *Hemi-Cuda* was redesigned around the large fastback rear glass by placing slots in the plexiglass backlight, allowing air to pass through and eliminating any negative pres-sure. The grille openings were blocked to prevent positive pressure under the front of the car. At the 1965 AHRA World Championship Meet at Lions Drag Strip in Long Beach, Califor-nia, the second *Hemi-Cuda* made its first wide-open-throttle pass on 65 percent nitro and turned 9.60/160.71. Eventually, the *Hemi-Cuda* would become the first funny to break the 180 mph mark.

The Commando 273 V–8 was rated at 235 hp at 5200 rpm. Air cleaner, oil filler and crankcase vent caps were chromed on the Commando 273. The valve covers were painted black with aluminum cooling fins.

Tom McEwen's Hemi-Cuda gets the once over from a half dozen inspectors. Sponsored by the Southern California Plymouth dealers, the Hemi-Cuda featured a 1,000 hp 426 Hemi parked behind the driver's seat. This was the first version, which crashed at 150 mph because of negative pressure at the backlight. The second version had holes drilled in the plexiglass backlight to eliminate the pressure pocket.

sporty car flair that had worked so well for the Corvair Monza. Sales took off, registering 64,596 units. While the Barracuda hardly put a dent in Mustang sales, it was gaining a reputation for good performance and handling. The

The Goldfish *was a steel-bodied 273 powered drag car sponsored by the Detroit-based Golden Commandos. The* Goldfish *won the F/Stock championship at the 1965 NHRA Nationals with a 13.47/103.68 mph.*

question was, how long would the fastback style remain in vogue?

1966: New Fins for the Fish

The Barracuda went into 1966 relatively unchanged. The rear received new taillamps and larger bumper, while up front the grille was revised, with a large, flat egg-crate design and massive front bumper. A pinstripe ran the full length of the car, and bright wheel-opening moldings were standard. The turn signal marker lamps were moved to the tops of the fenders. At the center of the bright molding below the rear glass was a new Barracuda emblem, styled by Antonick and depicting a swimming Barracuda.

Inside, the instrument panel was redesigned and was quite handsome, featuring six pods that contained all the instrumentation. On each side of the steering column was a large pod. The left

one housed a 120 mph speedometer on standard models and a 150 mph speedo when the Commando 273 V–8 was ordered. An engine vacuum gauge was installed in the right-hand pod unless the optional tachometer was ordered. At the 5 o'clock position under the right pod was the ignition switch. To the left of the speedometer was the fuel and engine temperature gauges. Below them were the headlamp and wiper switches. To the right of the tachometer (or standard vacuum gauge) were the oil pressure and ammeter gauges. Next to the gauges were the heater-defroster controls and just below, the optional radio.

The bucket seats were redesigned and offered more side bolster. Between the seats was a new, longer console that was offered with either a four speed or the automatic TorqueFlite. Plymouth dropped the Hurst shifter in place of a T-bar shifter that used a reverse lock-out lever. The fold-down rear seat and opening security panel were still standard, and Plymouth noted in 1966 that the "utility compartment is big enough to serve as sleeping quarters for fishermen, hunters and vacationing couples stop-

ping at state and national parks." Many teenagers also utilized the compartment for Saturday night submarine races.

The Barracuda's mechanicals were mostly unchanged for 1966. The Commando 273 remained the top powerplant, still rated at 235 hp. Front disc brakes were now a factory-installed option, as was fast-ratio, 16:1 manual steering. The Formula S Package was again offered, however for 1966 the buyer could order the same suspension package without the other components of the Formula S option.

Now in the third year of its styling cycle, the 1966 Barracuda was looking a little long in the tooth. Compared to the newly restyled Mustang and corporate cousin Dodge Charger, the Barracuda was too closely associated to the Valiant, and when held up next to the competition, its styling was noticeably dated. Sales reflected the Barracuda's stale image; only 38,029 units were sold in 1966.

Obviously it was time for a change, both in styling and drivetrains. The ponycar and musclecar market was rapidly moving away from the Euro-

While the thin blade bumper, split grilles with inset parking lamps design of 1964–1965 was attractive, it created cooling problems. To improve airflow to the radiator, an eggcrate grille was designed and the Valiant's front bumper was utilized, placing the parking lamps in the massive bumper. "This one cooled okay," recalls Antonick. "It just didn't look good." The Formula S Barracuda was equipped with the solid-lifter 273 ci V–8 that produced 235 hp. The Formula S shown here is without the racing stripe that ran across the top of the car from hood to rear bumper.

Ronnie Sox carries the front wheels as he launches his 1966 Barracuda funny car. Running a nitro-burning injected 426 Hemi, the front of the Sox and Martin Barracuda was stretched and the wheelbase altered. Sox's match races with Dyno Don Nicholson and his Eliminator I Comet were some of the most competitive of 1966. Sox turned a consistent 8.95/155.90. In September 1966 at Capital Raceway, Sox ran 8.72/167.59 against Phil Bonner's long-nose Mustang funny car.

Pee Wee Wallace in The Virginian *was a tough competitor in S/Ultimate Stock. The Barracuda was popular with racers thanks to its low weight and the mighty Chrysler Hemi engine, which dominated the Stock and Fuel classes.*

pean-inspired models of 1964–1965, and horsepower was now the key to image and sales. Chrysler watched as Ford mopped up the ponycar market and GM took control of the musclecar market. These two markets would begin to converge in 1967, and Chrysler would be ready with a new Barracuda.

1966 Accessory Groups
Basic Group
Radio, Transaudio Am push-button with antenna
Mirror, outside left, remote control
Mirror, inside, day/night

Sport Group (not offered with Formula S Package)
Steering wheel, simulated wood grain
Wheel covers, bolt-on wheel design
Tires, whitewall 7.00x13 in.

Suspension Package (not offered with Formula S Package)
Heavy-duty rear springs
Heavy-duty front torsion bars
Antisway bar

Formula S Package (not offered with Suspension Package or Sport Group)
Commando 273 4–bbl V–8 engine
Suspension Package
Firm Ride shock absorbers
Tachometer
6.95x13 in. Blue Streak tires
Heavy-gauge 14 in. wheels
Bolt-on-type wheel covers
Formula S nameplates

1966 Optional Equipment

Air conditioning
Bumper guards
California Cleaner Air Package
Console (not offered with three-speed manual transmission)
Rear window defogger (dealer installed)
Sure-Grip differential
Front disc brakes
Emergency flasher
Engine: 273 ci 4–bbl 235 hp (not offered with three-speed manual transmission)
Formula S Package
Tinted glass, all windows
Tinted glass, windshield only

Outside left-hand remote-control mirror
Day/night rearview mirror
Racing stripes
AM push-button radio with antenna
AM/FM push-button radio (dealer installed)
Retractable seat belts, front and rear
Wood-grained three-spoke steering wheel
Firm Ride shock absorbers
Tachometer (V–8 only)
Transmission: four-speed manual (V–8 only)
Three-speed TorqueFlite automatic
Trailer towing package
Undercoating with underhood insulation
Vinyl roof, black or white (not offered with racing stripes)
Wheel covers, bolt-on wheel design

Perhaps the most famous exhibition car of the 1960s was the Hurst Hemi Under Glass. Built by the "Shifty Doctor," Jack Watson, at Hurst's Research Center in Madison Heights, Michigan, the Hemi Under Glass could pop a wheelie that would last almost the entire length of the dragstrip. The 426 Hemi engine was mounted in the rear under the rear windows. When the Hemi Under Glass was first exhibited in 1965, the first wheelstands caused considerable damage to the rear bumper and sheetmetal. Watson then installed casters to reduce the height and angle of the wheelstands. First piloted by "Wild Bill" Shrewsberry, in 1966 Robert Riggle drove what Hurst nicknamed "The Aquarium."

The 1969 340 Formula S Barracuda convertible. The Formula S medallion was moved to
the taillamp panel in 1969 and a displacement
badge was located on the front fender below
the Barracuda script. Tom Glatch

Barracuda 1967–1969

Big Blocks and Drop Tops

As the musclecar and ponycar wars heated up in the fall of 1966, Plymouth introduced the 1967 Barracuda lineup on November 25, 1966. The past three years had allowed Plymouth's product planners to survey the field, and they recognized the dynamics of the market required an expanded product lineup that went beyond just one body style. It was time to realign the Barracuda, liberate it from the Valiant and beef up the engine lineup to compete in what was becoming a more lucrative—and competitive—marketplace.

Since the spring of 1964, Ford's Mustang had enjoyed a virtual lock on the sporty car and ponycar market. The Mustang was restyled for 1967 with more muscular looks and a powertrain to match. Thanks to a redesign of the engine bay that provided more space, Ford's thumping 390 ci engine was now available. Also new was the Mercury Cougar, an upscale cousin to the Mustang that also boasted an optional 390 engine.

This was also the year GM entered the game, releasing the 1967 Chevrolet Camaro in the fall of 1966. The Camaro was offered in a variety of performance levels, with a host of small-block engine choices and several versions of the legendary 396 cube Porcupine big-block, topped by the L78 engine, rated at 375 hp. Later in the model year, Pontiac would release the Firebird, with engines ranging from an innovative overhead-camshaft six-cylinder powerplant to a Ram Air 400.

To meet this kind of competition, Chrysler completely revamped the Barracuda for 1967. The Barracuda no longer shared the Valiant's platform, with the exception of wheelbase and the rear wheel inner, which, as Antonick recalls, "is the reason for the inverse wheel lips. When you put the coke bottle shape in that car, it put you out past the rear wheel inner. You weren't tying into it." Externally, essentially nothing else was shared with the Valiant.

1967: Lower, Lower, Wider

The second-generation Barracuda was new from the ground up. Three body styles were now offered: the signature fastback, a coupe and a convertible. It was a lineup identical to the Mustang.

Detroit's well-worn cliche of "lower, lower, wider" certainly applied to the new Barracuda as well. The wheelbase grew 2 in. to 108 in., while overall length stretched from 188.2 to 192.8 in. The Barracuda also gained a wider front track, measuring 57.4 in., up from 55.9 in. The rear track remained the same at 55.6 in. Width increased to 71.6 in. and overall height for the fastback was 53.4 in. for the fastback, 53.5 in. for the coupe and 54.1 in. for the convertible. The engine bay was also 2 in. wider—room that

Milt Antonick's original clay proposal for the 1967 Barracuda fastback. The Studebaker Avanti influence is obvious in this clay. Although it was turned down, this clay became quite influential both to Plymouth and

Dodge. Many of the styling elements in this October 1964 proposal eventually appeared on the 1966 Charger and 1967 Barracuda fastback.

The Barracuda SX show car influenced the final design of the 1967 Barracuda. The final form was in fiberglass with a non-functional chassis. Most of the SX styling was conceived by John Herlitz, who had only recently left GM to join Chrysler. Herlitz borrowed greatly from his time at GM for the SX, and when it hit the show circuit, it lead to a not-so-nice phone call from GM to the Plymouth design studio. The SX looks very GM from the cowl back, however Plymouth design was responsible for the grille. Both Dodge and Plymouth wanted the split grille theme, but Plymouth won out and utilized it for the 1967–1969 Barracuda.

The Plymouth design team studies the 1967 Barracuda fastback. From left to right: Dave Cummins, William Shannon, John Sampson, studio chief Richard McAdams, John Herlitz (in car), Jerald Thorley, Irv Ritchie and Milt Antonick, kneeling.

would come in handy as Plymouth began shoehorning bigger engines into the Barracuda.

The inspiration for the smooth, flowing lines of the second-generation Barracuda can be traced to European sports and grand touring cars. Plymouth designers picked a number of continental styling cues for the Barracuda, ranging from the chrome hood louvers to the fog lamp-style parking lamps mounted in the grilles.

For the most part, the 1967 Barracuda fastback was Milt Antonick's design, and some of the Avanti cues from his days working under Raymond Loewy at Studebaker also found their way onto the car. "There's a tie-in to the Avanti, especially the rear end shape of the car," Antonick said. "There is an S-shape to the sheetmetal and in that S-shape, the bumper resides and it doesn't touch the body. That's kind of my theme. I wanted to just let the bumper float completely free like the European cars. That's my European contribution to that car. The other thing is the bumper is one part front to rear. In other words, the planned view on the rear is the same as the front. It's the same piece, same part. I'm proud of that one."

The Barracuda's sheetmetal incorporated a large, flat hood that rolled to the fenders, with the line dropping off to rounded flanks. The design is smooth and devoid of sculpturing or excessive bright work. The Barracuda's trademark split-grille theme was carried over for 1967, with the grilles set into the openings and the parking lamps inset into the grilles. Block letters above the front header spelled out Plymouth, and a thin-line bumper floated below the grilles. Side glass was curved, and a gentle, Coke-bottle kick up to the rear quarters ended in a concave taillamp panel trimmed in matte-finished aluminum.

On fastback models, no longer did the backglass wrap around the C-pillar. Instead, it now laid flat, with less glass area. In profile, the fastback's C-pillars flowed cleanly into the deck. On coupe models the roofline was different, with a concave backlight that swept down to a long deck area. The effect was Italian.

The new convertible offered a power top and glass backlight.

Antonick's love of European cars—he had an Austin-Healey along with a Barracuda—inspired him to incorporate other European touches to the second-generation Barracuda. One special element was the pit stop gas cap.

"The Triumph TR3s and TR4s had the external snap-open gas cap, and it just seems like the right thing to do on a sports car," Antonick said. "I bought one of the Indy-type caps, a big, aluminum thing about 5 in. in diameter. When you snapped it, it made a hollow popping noise. I popped it and [Chief Designer Elwood] Engle saw it and said, let's put that on the car." The cap was mounted high on the quarter panel, increasing the vertical drop to the tank and decreasing the fill tube's intrusion into the interior compartment. Dodge would pick up Antonick's pit stop gas cap and use it on its new 1968 Charger a year later.

Another addition to the Barracuda's ornamentation in 1967 was "The Fish," a circular emblem with a stylized version of a Barracuda affixed to the front fenders, hood and rear deck. The fish had first appeared on a medallion in the center grille and in the center of the lower backglass bright molding in 1966. Antonick, who designed the emblem, recalls that "the profile of the fish was a Ferrari body side section, which is my favorite side section, a simple break. The break is about one third up, two thirds lower, one third up like a Ferrari. And it's a shark with a shark tail, and it's missing the Barracuda's forward dorsal fin. It's

The 1967 Barracuda Formula S fastback. Note the low placement of the reverse lamps and the large, single exhaust tip. This Formula S is equipped with optional headrests, redline tires and bolt-on style wheel covers.

A new addition to the Barracuda lineup for 1967 was the coupe. The graceful C-pillars and long rear deck attracted nearly as many buyers as the fastback. Also offered was a vinyl top for the coupe and fastback.

Rounding out the 1967 model lineup was a convertible with power top. The smooth lines of the 1967 Barracuda were complimented by the drop top. Notice the clean door cut out and the absence of other seams. A number of pinstripes and bolder stripe packages were offered on all models in 1967.

Formula S Package

The Formula S Package was again offered in 1967, however now the buyer could chose the 273 or 383 ci engine. The basic components of the successful Formula S road and handling package were retained from 1966. The heavy-duty front torsion bars were increased from 90 lb. per inch to 103 lb. per inch, and a large 0.88 in. front antiroll bar was added. Around back, the large six-leaf rear springs were stiffened to 136 lb. of deflection. Heavy-service shock absorbers with 1 in. pistons were installed along with D70x14 Red Streak tires on 5.5x14 in. stamped-steel wheels and Formula S medallions on the front fenders. These emblems had been designed by Dave Cummins, the designer of the first Valiant Fastback back in 1962.

If the 383 engine was specified in place of the 273, front disc brakes were mandatory and dual exhausts were standard. Special "383 Four Barrel" plaques were affixed to the front fenders.

The Formula S Package had proven itself in 1965 and 1966 as a superb road package, and specially prepared Formula S Bar-racudas again won the SCCA rally championship in 1967. The Formula S also competed against the Mustangs and Darts in the SCCA Trans-Am road race series. The 235 hp 273 cube engine in the coupe body was the best combination from a weight and handling standpoint.

Body Style	273	383
Fastback	2953 lb.	3205 lb.
Coupe	2868 lb.	3120 lb.
Convertible	2973 lb.	3225 lb.

(All weights shown are shipping weights)

Most of the added weight of the 383 rested over the front wheels, adding more understeer to the car's handling. Although the 273 powered coupe would have a slight disadvantage with its lower power-to-weight ratio, the 273 equipped Formula S would be more nimble in the corners thanks to better weight distribution. Of course, on the drag strip the 383, competing in C/Stock, would be competitive with the 390 Mustang, running in the low to mid 15s at 90–93 mph.

The Barracuda's cockpit was also all new for 1967. Shown here are the optional headrests, console and full-ring steering wheel. On manual transmission models, Chrysler continued to use its own shifter instead of the popular Hurst unit.

more like a pike. Actually, it's a combination of a shark, a pike and a Ferrari body side. I was supposed to do research on it, but I didn't. I already knew what I wanted."

The European influence was also apparent in the Barracuda's interior. The instrument panel was revised for 1967, and the gauge cluster was enlarged. Optional in the center was a "Performance Indicator," which was actually a vacuum gauge. This gauge could be replaced by an optional tachometer. On

Pre-production photo of the instrument cluster showed optional 150 mph speedometer and 6000 rpm tach incorrectly marked "Performance Indicator."

The 1967 273 Commando engine cranked out 235 hp thanks to a high-lift, mechanical cam, good heads and Carter four-barrel carburetor.

The Barracuda grew some teeth in 1967 thanks to the addition of the 383. Rated at 280 hp, the 383 Barracuda could turn mid 14s at 97 mph.

either side of the center instrument pod was the speedometer with trip odometer on the left and gauge package containing fuel gauge, oil pressure gauge, ampere gauge and water temperature gauge to the right. If the optional decor package was ordered, the 150 mph Rallye speedometer was installed.

The instrument panel was finished in pebble grain and brushed aluminum, with the emergency flashers and headlamps switches to the far left of the panel and the windshield wiper and washer to the right of the gauges. The heater control panel, located in the center of the dash, was placed directly above the radio.

Standard forward seating for the closed models was a bench seat with center armrest. Buckets were standard on the convertible and optional on the closed models. A center console was optional when bucket seats were specified, and if ordered, the TorqueFlite shifter was located in the console, as was the manual gearbox shifter.

The fold-down rear seat was again standard on all fastback Barracudas, however the release mechanism was redesigned and less obtrusive than the previous design. The trunk compartment could also be opened as in the past, providing a huge carpeted area for utility use. The coupe and convertible models had a standard trunk, with the spare located beneath a false floor, providing a large luggage area, unusual in most ponycars.

Plymouth product planners had been content to offer the Slant Six and the 318

V–8 as the only engine choices, however the news that Ford was to drop the 390 into the Mustang forced the introduction of the 383 into the Barracuda. In all, there were a total of four engines offered in 1967, starting with the base Slant Six, rated at 145 hp. A 273 cube V–8, rated at 180 hp was the other standard engine choice. On the option list was the Commando 273, pretty much a carryover from 1966, rated at 235 hp.

The top gun was the new Commando 383, downrated from the usual 325 hp to 280 hp at 4200 due mostly to a milder camshaft and restrictive exhaust manifolds, required by the close quarters of the Barracuda's engine compartment. Torque was an impressive 400 lb-ft at 2400 rpm. A Carter four-barrel fed the 10.25:1 compression engine a diet of premium fuel, and dual exhausts with low restriction mufflers were standard with the 383.

35

It didn't take long for drag racers to begin using the new body style on the track. Butch Leal was one of the first to campaign the new Barracuda. Leal's funny Barracuda ran an injected 426 Hemi.

The 383 was offered only with four speed or TorqueFlite with console-mounted shifter; disc brakes were also a mandatory option. And even with the extra 2 in. in the new engine bay, accommodations were so tight that the power steering pump had to be redesigned to clear the exhaust manifold. Air conditioning was absolutely out of the question.

For the rest of the engine lineup, three transmissions were offered: a three-speed manual with the shifter mounted on the column, the A–833 four-speed with floor-mounted shifter and the three-speed TorqueFlite automatic with either console- or column-mounted shifter. Rear gears ranged from 2.93:1 to 3.23:1 with the 7.25 in. ring gear, while heavier service requirements and Sure-Grip limited-slip differential applications in 3.23:1. 3.55:1 and 3.91:1 ratios all used a stouter 8.75 in. ring gear.

Beneath the new skin, the Barracuda retained the same basic chassis, suspension and brakes as in previous models, however there were a number of improvements. At the rear, additional leaves were added to the springs when the 383 engine or heavy-duty suspension was ordered. Wheel diameters were increased to 14 in. and 6.95x14 blackwall

or optional whitewall tires were used on Slant Six and 273 applications. Optional on all engines (or standard with the 383 engine), when air conditioning or air conditioning and front disc brakes was ordered, was a Red Streak D70x14 performance tire.

On V–8 cars, 10 in. drum brakes were standard at all four corners. Four-piston disc brakes with large 10.79 in. cast-iron rotors were optional, but standard when the 383 engine was ordered.

For the most part, the new Barracuda lineup received good press from the car magazines, and sales improved over 1966. While it could be said the new line of three body styles and a new engine should have created higher sales numbers than 62,534, in the face of new introductions from Pontiac, Chevrolet,

The famous Hurst Hemi Under Glass was rebodied in 1967 and still performed its incredible wheelies from the starting line to the traps.

Mercury and a restyled Mustang, the Barracuda retained an important share of the ponycar market. Within Plymouth, the Barracuda was outsold only by

In an attempt to improve engine cooling, Plymouth designers experimented with the Barracuda's split grille. This attempt to improve engine cooling by enlarging the grille area included this hidden headlamp proposal. The theme was carried to the rear of the car with four horizontal taillamps.

For 1968, the Barracuda lineup was little changed. Wire wheel covers were now available. The simulated mag wheel covers on the coupe were first introduced in 1967. Sport stripes and decor packages were also added in 1968.

the Fury III and the Valiant, and accounted for approximately 10 percent of total Plymouth sales in 1967.

1968: Refining the Fish

Since 1967 had been the year for new sheetmetal, 1968 was a year of refine-

The 1968 hardtop decked out with the 340 Formula S package, wire wheel covers, sports stripe and headrests. To meet Federal requirements, side marker lamps were now required at the front fenders and rear quarters.

The 1968 Barracuda convertible. Note the hood ornaments with no engine designation. These blank ornaments were used with six-cylinder or 318 engine applications. The fish emblem beneath the Barracuda script on the fender included a V–8 identifier when the 318 was installed. With six-cylinder cars only the fish resided in the emblem.

There was little change to the Barracuda's interior for 1968. When the optional Rallye Instrument Cluster was ordered, a 150 mph speedometer was installed along with a trip odometer and the dash was covered with a wood-grained applique. Also shown here is the three-spoke, simulated wood-grained steering wheel.

The Interior Decor Group added a touch of luxury to the Barracuda's apointments. Included in the package were map pouches and simulated wood-grained trim on the doors, special seat upholstery, rear seat armrest with ashtrays, bright trim on all pedals and carpeted rear wheelhouses on fastbacks.

ment for the Barracuda. "The first year," recalls Antonick, "when you go through and design the body, it's really difficult to come in the second and third year and really improve on it."

Instead, 1968 was the year Chrysler Engineering rolled out the new 340, a dazzling gem of a small-block that was the perfect match for the sporty Barracuda. While the 383 provided lots of torque, it was a tight fit in the Barracuda's engine bay and wasn't offered with air conditioning. Thanks to the smaller bulk of the 340, the spark plugs were easy to reach, air conditioning was offered and enthusiasts quickly discovered that winding the 340 out in the top three gears was as much fun as laying down long streaks of rubber in first. The 340 transformed the Barracuda into a street sizzler to do battle with small-block Camaros. Gone was the 273 and the 318 was now the base V–8 engine, with the 340 the standard engine with the Formula S Package.

The 340 Barracuda soon gained a reputation for performance and with the Formula S Package, the 'Cuda (as it was starting to be called in slang on the street) was transformed into a legitimate high-performing grand touring car. Along with the 383, the 340 gave the Barracuda a one-two product punch that was tough to beat on the boulevard.

The 340 was new from the ground up, and while it shared some basic engineering with the other members of the LA engine family (273 and 318), the 340 was designed to provide excellent torque response across the rpm range. Its combustion-chamber design also lent itself to more efficient burning of hydrocarbons, an important factor as Detroit struggled to meet new federal emissions regulations.

Weighing just 539 lb. dry, the 340 shared the LA family's stroke of 3.31 in. With a bore size of 4.04 in., however, the 340 produced approximately 15 percent more power than the 273 four-barrel for 275 hp at 5000 rpm and 340 lb-ft of torque at 3200 rpm. Much of this improvement was due to an extremely efficient head design, with large intake and exhaust ports. Chrysler's advertised horsepower of the 340 was somewhat underrated; the NHRA refactored the 340's output at 290 hp.

Thin wall castings of the block provided much of the weight savings. A drop-forged crank was used, and with the high-rpm applications of the 340, a windage tray was placed between the crank and the oil pump to prevent oil cavitation and loss of horsepower. The rods were heavier forgings than the 273 or 318, and the notched, flat-top pistons were aluminum alloy with a compression ratio of 10.75:1.

Two camshafts were available, depending on transmission choice. Stick shift-equipped 340s featured cams with a duration of 276 degrees and 0.445 in. lift at intake and 284 degrees and 0.455 in. lift on the exhaust with 52 degrees of overlap. With the TorqueFlite, the cam carried 268 degrees of intake with 0.430 in. lift and 276 degrees exhaust with 0.445 in. lift with 44 degrees of valve overlap. Both cams used hydraulic lifters and solid 0.28 in. pushrods. The large valves of 2.02 in. intake and 1.60 in. exhaust used heavy-duty springs and surge dampers.

A dual-plane cast-iron intake manifold was fed by a Carter AVS (air valve-controlled secondaries) carburetor topped by an unsilenced air cleaner. The AVS featured primary bores of 1.44 in. and secondaries of 1.69 in. with a straight bore and no venturis. Spark was provided by a dual-breaker distributor.

The remainder of the 1968 package was mostly a carryover from 1967 with

some minor trim and mechanical changes. "We added some bold items on the car," noted Antonick. "The

stripes were a little bolder, the wheel covers became a little bolder. We seemed to have been trying to take a

So you're coming up to the Christmas tree and the exhaust is going *bappetybappety-bappetybappety* and all those little internal bits are going *whumpawhumpawhumpawhump* and you're out to grind the sound barrier into bite-sized equations with your howlin' Barracuda.
Say what? BARRACUDA? You're kidding! Nope. And this is why:
A new, lightweight, high-winding 340 cubic incher you can order. Its strength lies in things like intake valve diameters of 2.02 inches and exhaust diameters of 1.60 inches. Then there's the cam, which goes in 4-speed cars and is definitely of the

"let's do it" variety: .445 inch lift on intake and .455 inch on exhaust, with 60 degrees of overlap. Intake duration is 284 degrees with 292 degrees on exhaust. The resultant idle is so wild an automatic box can't quite cope with it. Hence, the cam you get with TorqueFlite models is a bit less hairy. The score: 275 bhp @ 5,000 rpm.
As if that isn't enough, we have another engine option, this one with 383 cubic inches. For openers, the heads are new and have big 2.3 inch ports. The intake valves are 2.08 inches in diameter and the exhausts are 1.74. The cam provides a .425 inch lift on intake and .437 on exhaust.

Overlap is 40 degrees; duration is 264 degrees, intake, and 268 degrees, exhaust. For a total of 300 bhp @ 4,200 rpm. And *much* torque.
In either case, Barracuda is one running organization—a natural for sanctioned drag racing.
And just to show how we feel about sanctioned drags, we'll pay you to do your racing there. Any Plymouth that takes Stock Eliminator at a NHRA National or Regional gets a cash contingency award from us. You won't get rich from it, but it helps. Sort of makes safety pay.
...the Plymouth win-you-over beat goes on. ♥

Write for four 24 in. x 17 in. full-color cartoon posters of GTX, Road Runner and Barracuda (shown below). Send $1.00 to: Posters, P.O. Box 7749, Detroit, Mich. 48211.

Shortcut.

Plymouth CHRYSLER MOTORS CORPORATION

Plymouth Styling was called in to create a special hood scoop for the Hemi Barracuda. This version was carefully molded into the hood. It was rejected in favor of a tall scoop that was grafted to a fiberglass hood.

The Barracuda's advertising took a different tack beginning in 1968. Not only were the colorful and cartoonish renderings of the car exciting, but the copy grabbed young readers and held their eyeballs to the page: "So you're coming up to the Christmas tree and the exhaust is going bappetybappetybap-petybappety *and all those little internal parts are going* whumpawhumpawhumpawhum-pawhump *and you're out to grind the sound*

barrier into bite-sized equations with your howlin' Barracuda. Say what? BARRACUDA? You're kidding!" This was heady stuff for a car line that only months before was singing the virtues of European styling and road rallys. Thanks to the exciting new powertrains and youth-oriented advertising, beginning in 1968 the Barracuda gained new respect as a serious street performance car.

One of the most sanitary of the funny cars was Lime Fire, a one-piece body 1968 Barracuda owned by Jim St. Clair and driven by Clare Sanders. The 1,980 lb. fuel-burning dragster was powered by an injected 1958 Imperial Hemi cranking 1,500 hp. In this match race at Bristol, Sanders is about to dethrone Ed "The King" Schartman's Cyclone.

Tales of the Tape

By 1968, the ponycar market was getting crowded, and every player had a variety of engines to offer. The Barracuda's two performance engine choices covered the field beautifully.

How well did the 1968 Barracuda stack up against the competition? Check the results of a comparison test conducted by *Motor Trend* in January 1968:

	Barracuda	Camaro	Firebird	Javelin	Mustang
Engine	340	396	400	343	390
Horsepower	275 @ 5000	325 @ 4800	335 @ 5000	280 @ 4800	335 @ 4800
Torque	340 @ 3200	410 @ 3200	430 @ 3400	365 @ 3000	427 @ 3200
Transmission	3-spd auto	3-spd auto	3-spd auto	4-spd man	3-spd auto
Rear axle	3.23:1	3.07:1	3.90:1	3.15:1	3.25:1
Performance					
0–30 mph	3.2 sec.	3.2 sec.	2.8 sec.	3.2 sec.	3.0 sec
0–45 mph	5.3 sec.	5.0 sec.	5.0 sec.	5.0 sec.	5.1 sec
0–60 mph	8.1 sec.	7.8 sec.	7.6 sec.	7.6 sec.	7.8 sec.
Quarter-mile	15.2/92 mph	15.6/92 mph	15.4/93 mph	15.1/93 mph	15.2/94 mph

Compared to the big-block Camaro, Ram Air II Firebird and 390 Mustang, the 340 Barracuda was able to hold its own, and in the quarter-mile actually beat the Camaro and Firebird—and was as quick as the Mustang.

The fish also grew hair in 1968, thanks to a shoehorn job conjured up by Tom Hoover at Chrysler engineering. Hoover greased up the 426 Hemi and slipped it into the Barracuda's small engine bay. It was a tight fit but it turned the Barracuda into a ground pounding Super Stocker, clipping the quarter in less than 11 sec. at more than 130 mph.

very subtle but sophisticated design and do what everyone else was doing, jazzing it up just a bit."

Externally, the hood ornaments were redesigned, with six-cylinder or 318 equipped cars having a plain ornament. With either the 340–S or 383–S packages, the displacement was badged within the ornament.

The grille now featured a vertical treatment. The Plymouth nameplate was moved over to above the left-hand grille, and side marker lamps front and rear were now standard. Around back, the taillamps were restyled, and the reverse lamps were concealed within the taillamps.

On Formula S Packages, tire size was increased to E70x14. Four wheel cover styles were offered, the deluxe, bolt-on, mag style (which was dealer installed) or a wire wheel disc. The lower rocker molding was also new.

Inside, the instrument panel layout was virtually unchanged from 1967. The radio knobs were redesigned to a thumbwheel style. Seat upholstery was redone, as were the door and quarter trim panels.

Mechanical changes were few for 1968. The 383 was bumped from 280 to 300 hp at 5000 rpm, thanks to a new set of heads that boasted larger, 2.30 in. ports and larger exhaust valves. Transmission and rear-axle ratios were the same as 1967, as were the front and rear suspension and brakes.

1968 Hemi Barracuda
It was inevitable that Chrysler would build the Hemi Barracuda. For the past four years, drag racers had been gutting Barracudas and dropping in 392 or 426 Elephant Engines. Since Chrysler had enjoyed tremendous success on the dragstrips in Super Stock and Unlimited Fuel since 1963, the decision to continue that domination by building a factory super stocker (with some assistance from Hurst) was a natural.

The S/S Hemi Barracuda was assembled by Chrysler as a package and then shipped to Hurst. Although the number varies from source to source, at least fifty and possibly as many as seventy-five Barracudas were shipped to Hurst's facility in Detroit. The conversions were coordinated by Dick Maxwell at Chrysler and Richard Chrysler at Hurst. As delivered to the dealers, the cars had fiberglass hoods and fenders, while the front bumper and doors were light-gauge steel. The interiors were gutted and Bostrom driver seats installed.

To squeeze the mighty Elephant into the Barracuda's tight engine bay, some modifications had to be made under the hood. The battery was moved to the trunk, and the right shock tower was moved, as was the master cylinder. Hurst also installed custom headers, shift linkages for four-speed cars and special rear-axle assemblies. Off the transport trailer the cars were delivered on street tires. All that was needed to make the car competitive was slicks, a deeper oil pan

A 1968 Super Stock Hemi Barracuda, conceived by factory Ramcharger drag race team member Dick Maxwell. The prototype for the limited-production run was constructed by Chrysler and the cars were built by Hurst Performance. David Gooley

The 426 race Hemi was a snug fit in the engine bay of the 1968 Super Stock Barracuda. The Hemi breathed through a pair of four-barrel carburetors and Chrysler's special race manifold. David Gooley

(a small pan was installed for shipping), camshaft and valvetrain.

The S/S Hemi Barracudas were delivered to racers in early May, in time to qualify for the NHRA Spring Nationals. Ronnie Sox was one of the first to get a Hemi Barracuda on the strip and turned mid 10s right out of the box.

The introduction of the S/S Hemi Barracudas created controversy in the stock ranks, where the little guy now found himself pitted against national record holders in factory-built race cars. On February 20, 1968, Chrysler-Plymouth general sales manager R. D. McLaughlin outlined for dealers—and racers—what they could order. The following is a reprint of his letter in its entirety.

February 20, 1968
To: All Plymouth Dealers
Subject: 1968 Hemi Barracuda Super Stock

The Chrysler-Plymouth Division offers for the 1968 models a 426 Hemi-Powered Barracuda Fastback for use in supervised acceleration trials. These cars will weigh approximately 3,000 pounds and have been designed to meet the 1968 specifications of the major sanctioning drag strip organizations.

The Hemi-Powered Barracudas will be available through production in limited quantities in March. To order this vehicle, use the Barracuda Order Form and specify Body Code B029 and Transmission Code, either 4 Speed Manual, Code 393, or Automatic, Code 395. No other specifications are necessary.

Description of Components
— 426 cu. in. 8–cylinder engine with dual 4–barrel carburetors—12.5 to 1 compression ratio.
— Cross Ram intake manifold.
— $1\frac{11}{16}'' \times 1\frac{11}{16}''$ Holley carburetors.
— Competition Hooker headers, exhaust pipes, and mufflers.
— High capacity oil pump.
— Roller timing chain (reduced timing chain stretch for more consistent engine performance).
— Mechanical valve gear.
— Dual breaker distributor.
— Transistor ignition.
— Metal core type ignition wires.
— Unsilenced air cleaners.
— Deep groove fan drive pulleys.
— Heavy duty radiator.
— Aluminum seven-blade fan equipped with Viscous drive.
— Special offset 15" rear wheels.
— Chrysler-built 8¾" large stem pinion gear set, and heavy-duty axle shafts with automatic transmission (4.86 axle ratio).
— Dana-built 9¾" heavy-duty axle with manual transmission (4.88 axle ratio).
— Sure-Grip differential.
— 135 Amp. hr. battery (located in rear compartment).
— Heavy-duty high control rear suspension.
— Front disc brakes 4½" Bolt Circle.
— Fiberglass front fenders.
— Fiberglass hood with scoop.
— Light weight steel doors.
— Light weight front bumper.
— Light weight side window glass.
— High capacity fuel lines.
— Business coupe interior (2 bucket seats—no rear seat).

For Manual Transmission Only
— Special heavy-duty 10½" clutch and flywheel.
— Safety steel clutch housing.

— Competition "Slick Shift" 4–speed transmission.
— Hurst remote mounted floor-shift unit with reverse lockout.

For Automatic Transmission Only

— High stall speed torque converter (large drive lugs and $\frac{7}{16}$" diameter attaching screws).
— Heavy-duty manual shift TorqueFlite transmission.
— Hurst floor-mounted shift unit.

Please Note:

The following items are deleted on this body type:
Heater, Body Sealer and Sound Deadeners, Silencing Pads, Outside Mirrors, Right Side Seat Belt, and Body Color Paint.

NO OPTIONAL EQUIPMENT OF ANY KIND CAN BE ORDERED.

The policy of Chrysler Corporation is one of continual improvement in design and manufacture, wherever possible, to insure a still finer car. Hence, specifications, equipment and prices are subject to change without notice.

These vehicles are intended to use in supervised acceleration trials and other competitive events, therefore, they will be sold *without warranty.* Special stickers will be provided for plant installation (attached to left "A" post) which will read as follows: "This vehicle was not manufactured for use on public streets, roads or highways and does not conform to Motor Vehicle Safety Standards."

All customer orders must be accompanied by a signed disclaimer (sample attached) indicating that the purchaser understands that this vehicle is sold *without warranty* and does not conform to Federal Vehicle Safety Standards.

Any prospective customer who desires to purchase one of these maximum performance vehicles should be made aware of the following characteristics which make them unsuitable for general use.

1. A high idle speed is required to insure adequate lubrication, minimize roughness, and to keep the engine from stalling.
2. The modified intake manifold causes a rich surging condition, misfiring and unstable engine operation in cold weather, which makes ordinary street driving extremely difficult and it is not recommended for this use.
3. Higher than normal oil consumption will be encountered because of increased lubrication to the valve train and cylinder walls.
4. The carburetors are calibrated for maximum power and a high numerical axle ratio is used for good acceleration. As a result, the gas mileage is considerably less than for a conventional car.
5. Engine noise would be objectionable due to increased piston clearance and mechanical valve tappet clearance.
6. The ignition system is designed for optimum engine output and must be kept in top condition. This makes it necessary to inspect, adjust and replace the spark plugs and ignition points more frequently than would be necessary on a standard engine.
7. On cars equipped with automatic transmission, band adjustment must be made frequently.
8. Due to performance characteristics, maintenance and operating expense will be high since premium fuel is required and frequent oil changes are a MUST.
9. Does not conform to Motor Vehicle Safety Standards.

Warranty and Policy Coverage

Any customer purchasing this model vehicle should be advised that due to the expected use, the vehicle is sold "as is" and the 24 month or 24,000 mile vehicle warranty coverage, the 5 year or 50,000 mile Power Train Warranty coverage, or any other warranty coverage (including, but not limited to the implied warranties of fitness for purpose intended or merchantability) will *not* apply to the vehicle. The manufacturer assumes no responsibility for the manner in which such vehicles operate.

Any repairs or adjustments which you believe warrant factory participation should be brought to the attention of your Regional Service Office where such requests will be handled on individual merits.

Attached is a form letter (to be prepared on your letterhead) which should be thoroughly understood and signed by each prospective purchaser and attached to your order for each Hemi Barracuda Super Stock. The purpose of the letter is to explain the normal operation characteristics of these vehicles and clarify that the warranty coverages *do not* apply. Be sure a letter in this form, signed by your customer, is included with your order so there will be no delay.

1969: Arrival of the 'Cuda

The ponycar wars were at their height in late 1968 as Detroit prepared to trot out its 1969 offerings. The distinction between musclecars and ponycars had now blurred in the eyes of the enthusiasts. Where before there had been an emphasis on handling and the "sports car" image, now the car makers' focus had shifted to gut-wrenching powerplants in excess of 400 cubes that were absolute torque monsters on the street. The power-to-weight benefit gained by dropping a big engine into an even smaller car was not missed by Ford, who in 1968 drew the most attention with its new 428 Mustang. By 1969, ponycars were entering a new plateau in performance.

All of this activity was not missed by the insurance companies, who were writing policies on these cars and adding stifling premium surcharges (as high as 100 percent) to the very drivers these

The Wheel That Wasn't

Chrysler's first attempt at a lightweight aluminum road wheel was introduced at the beginning of the 1969 model year. Identified as option code W23, the two-piece wheel consisted of a cast-aluminum-alloy center with a steel rim and a bright trim ring. Option W23 was offered in 14 and 15 in. diameters to fit virtually the entire Dodge and Plymouth product lineup.

Immediately after introduction, problems began occurring with the aluminum wheel. Engineering tests indicated the lug nuts would loosen during operation. Torquing them down resulted in cracking the aluminum-alloy center. Chrysler was determined to get the wheels off all cars to prevent any accidents. If the lug nuts worked themselves loose, the possibility existed that a wheel could come off, causing the driver to lose control of the vehicle. The resulting lawsuits against Chrysler would cost the corporation millions of dollars in judgments and legal fees.

By the first week of September 1968, notices went out to all dealers that if they had any cars in stock built before August 28 with the W23 option, it was "mandatory that all aluminum cast road wheels be replaced before delivery of the vehicle." The Regional Sales Offices contacted dealers with factory-supplied lists of cars built with the W23 option. Some of the cars on the list had their wheels changed at the factory; however, dealers with cars equipped with the cast wheels were required to supply their Regional Office with a list of the vehicle serial numbers and the status of each car as replacement wheels were installed.

Because Chrysler so resolutely collected the W23 wheels before they were released, almost no examples exist today.

Somehow some wheels did get out, and today they can be found on show cars or at swap meets. Valued in the thousands of dollars, the W23 road wheels were Chrysler's first—and last—attempt at exotic lightweight alloy wheels until the 1980s.

The ill-fated aluminum wheels were pulled at the last moment because the lug nuts would not remain tight. Today they are rare collectibles.

Blame it on the excesses of the times or simply bad taste. The Mod Top Floral Vinyl Roof and Floral Vinyl Trim were offered for the Barracuda in yellow and black only beginning September 9, 1968.

The sports stripe package was offered in either red, white or black and was available with the 340 or the 383 engine.

"Mr. Four Speed" Ronnie Sox continued to campaign his 1968 426 Hemi in 1969. At the 1969 Spring Nationals, Sox cleaned house in Super Stock with a 10.63.

cars were aimed at—single males under the age of 25, the highest risk segment of the driving public. These high premiums were beginning to slowly push the price of admission to new musclecars beyond the grasp of many young adults.

To the legions of safety advocates (many of which were funded by the insurance industry), the very existence of high-performance cars was unacceptable to the public's welfare. Citing accident charts, statistics and Detroit's own methods for advertising high-performance cars, safety advocates demanded Detroit stop building musclecars. When legislators in Washington

began looking into the matter, Detroit quickly abandoned the high-performance market.

All of this was to take place after 1969, but at the end of the decade, the stage was already being set for the demise of the high-performance car. What no one in Detroit understood or anticipated was that enthusiasts would make themselves heard less than ten years later.

Plymouth's response to the spiraling performance market was to field two new models in the 1969 Barracuda lineup, the 'Cuda 340 and the 'Cuda 383. The Cuda series were easily recognized by twin, matte black hood scoops atop matching black hood tape strips. The tape stripes also appeared along the rocker panels, and tape "callouts" (engine displacement emblems) were located on the lower front fenders behind the wheel openings.

Next page
The Barracuda's profile was enhanced with the convertible model. Factory records indicate eighty-three 340–S convertibles were shipped in 1969. Tom Glatch

Although the 'Cuda shared many components with the Formula S Package, the 'Cuda was inspired by the Plymouth Road Runner. The 'Cuda was for street racing, while the Formula S was for the sophisticated driver who appreciated handling. At least, that was the strategy.

The 'Cuda series also packed some heavy hardware. Plymouth chose to return to the Hurst shifter on four-speed transmission versions; however, the bulletproof Hurst linkage was replaced with a cheaper set of shift rods that were soon discarded by 'Cuda owners in favor

49

of Hurst's equipment. A heavy-duty suspension and E70x14 tires were also standard.

The 340 engine was virtually unchanged for 1969. The 383, on the other hand, was pumped up to 330 hp, thanks mostly to a more severe camshaft with 0.450 in. lift on intake and 0.465 in. lift on exhaust. This new stick allowed the 383 to produce peak horsepower at 5200 rpm and maximum torque of 410 lb-ft at 3600 rpm.

In April 1969, Plymouth released the 440 'Cuda. Based on the 383 platform, the 375 hp 440 was a snug fit in the 'Cuda's engine bay but turned the 'Cuda into a rocket, achieving 0–60 mph acceleration in 5.6 sec. and clicking off box-stock quarter-mile times of 14.10/104 mph. The 440 'Cuda was offered strictly for straight-line performance, and since accommodations under the hood were tight, power brakes, power steering, disc brakes and air conditioning were not available.

Driving the 440 'Cuda without power steering was guaranteed to produce massive biceps. With a ratio of 19.15:1, when the 440 'Cuda was pushed into a corner the slow manual steering made it difficult to control the huge amounts of understeer. Equally missed were disc brakes and power assist. Only one transmission—the three-speed Torque-Flite—was offered. Two rear-axle ratios were on the books, a 3.55:1 or 3.91:1, both with the Sure-Grip 8¾ in. Dana rear.

If the 440 'Cuda was apt to bludgeon the boulevard, the 340 Formula S caressed the road. By 1969, the 340 Formula S had been completely refined, with tuned suspension, larger tires and superb brakes. Offered with power discs and power steering, the 340 Formula S was truly a driver's car. It stands today as one of the most sophisticated—and least appreciated—sporty cars of the 1960s.

The Barracuda interior was mostly unchanged for 1969. Buyers could opt for the Interior Decor Group, which offered special upholstery for the front bucket seats and bucket-styled rear seat, wood-grain inserts on the instrument panel, door and quarter trim panels, map pouches on the doors, bright trim

The 1969 Barracuda fastback. This particular owner chose to shod his 340-S with a set of 1970 Rally wheels.

Bucket seats were standard; however, the console-mounted automatic shifter was optional.

on the pedals, rear seat armrests with ashtrays and carpeted rear wheelhouses in the fastback. The folding rear seat was now optional in the fastback and mandatory with the Decor Group.

Plymouth sales continued to decline and the Barracuda suffered along with the rest of the model lineup. Final production totals were 12,757 coupes, 1,442 convertibles and 17,788 fastbacks. It was obvious that the Barracuda was in need of a total redesign to remain competitive. In the six model years since the first Barracuda of 1964, the market had changed from the sporty car in-spired by the Corvair Monza Spyder and defined by the Ford Mustang to ground-pounding, big-cube musclecars still de-fined as "ponycars" only by virtue of their wheelbase and basic styling.

With the end of the 1969 model year, the Barracuda marked the end of its second generation. It had never matched the sales performance of the Mustang and the Camaro; however, the

---

'Cuda 440

The 'Cuda 440 was introduced in the spring of 1969 as a limited-edition package. All 440 'Cudas were two-door hardtops. Factory documents indicate all were equipped with console-mounted TorqueFlites and 3.55:1 or 3.91:1 Sure-Grip limited-slip rear axles with 8¾ in. ring gears. Power brakes, power steering, disc brakes and air conditioning were not offered. All 440 'Cudas can be identified as BS23M9B or BS29M9B in the VIN number.

Mechanically, the 440 'Cudas used the 383 engine's oil pan, oil pump suction pipe and strainer. The left-hand exhaust manifold was unique to the 440 'Cuda, as was the left front engine support bracket and the throttle cable. The remainder of the package utilized components from the 'Cuda 383.

Chrysler knew these cars were going to be used for more than occasional trips to the grocery store, so the driveshaft, universal joints, rear axle and differential were not covered by warranty. The engine and transmission were covered for twelve months or 12,000 miles.

Rated at 375 hp at 4600 rpm and a thumping 480 lb-ft of torque at 3200 rpm, the 440 'Cuda was designed for one thing: straight-line acceleration. *Super Stock and Drag Illustrated* drove one to 13.89/103.2.

Barracuda had proven to be a profitable product for Chrysler. And even though the storm clouds of safety and insurance were gathering on the horizon, Chrysler prepared to enter the 1970 model year with new, aggressive products, projecting that the next generation of Barracudas (and its new Dodge cousin) would enlarge Chrysler's share of the musclecar and ponycar market.

The lingering fear in the minds of some Chrysler product planners was that the market was already in a tailspin

The standard fold-down rear seat that had become the Barracuda fastback's trademark became optional in 1969.

In its final year of production, Plymouth produced 17,788 Barracuda fastbacks, 1,431 equipped with the 340-S package.

The 1969 340-S was extremely competitive on the dragstrip. Hot Rod recorded quarter-mile performance of 14.32/99.7.

Not all Formula S Barracudas came decked out in stripes. It was also popular to order your muscle incognito, making it easier to suck the chrome off unknowing competition.

56

from which there was no recovery. If so, then Chrysler's new generation of ponycars were too late for the party.

While the hardtop coupe had initially been a strong seller hot on the heels of the fastback, by 1969 it had fallen behind. Only 325 340-S hardtop coupes were shipped by Plymouth in 1969.

The small-block 340 was a screamer, producing 275 hp at 5000 rpm and 340 lb-ft of torque at 3200 rpm. With its silky torque range and high-rpm capability, the Commando 340 was one of the finest high-performance engines of the musclecar era.

Chrysler wisely chose to return to Hurst shifters for use with manual transmission models. The good Hurst shifter arms were substituted with cheaper units, however. Note the radio delete plate in the instrument panel. The fire extinguisher was installed by the owner.

The optional Interior Decor Group also included special upholstery for the front and rear seats. The three-spoke wood-grained sport steering wheel was also optional. Tom Glatch

Even with accessories like power brakes and power steering, there was still plenty of room in the close quarters of the Barracuda's engine bay when the 340 was installed. Tom Glatch

Dodge also entered the 1970 SCCA Trans-Am circuit and the 340 T/A Challenger homologated the race version for competition. The Challenger T/A hood was fiberglass with a large "pursuit plane" style hood scoop. Mechanically, the 340 T/A and the AAR 'Cuda were virtually identical.

Barracuda and Challenger 1970–1974

Rise and Fall of the Chrysler Ponycar

Development of the next generation Barracuda began in February of 1967 in Chrysler's Advanced Styling Studios under the supervision of Cliff Voss. It was here in Advanced Styling that the main themes for the 1970 Barracuda would be determined in conjunction with the Advanced Planning and Advanced Engineering groups. With the shift in emphasis from sporty to muscle, there was considerable pressure from top management to get the new platform right. The platform was to be called the E-body.

For Engineering, there was one absolute: the new E-body engine compartment had to be large enough to accept engines up to 440 ci along with air conditioning, power steering, power brakes and other accessories. The ponycar had also become musclecar, and in a market where there was no replacement for displacement—and where before the Barracuda had always come up short—Chrysler was determined that no one was going to have a more potent engine lineup.

To achieve this goal, the cowl from the larger B-body was assimilated into the design, permitting a large engine compartment. Advanced Styling was responsible for the area between the wheels, the "center section" of the car that housed the passengers. Voss' group set the guidelines for wheelbase, greenhouse, tumblehome, position of the sideglass and door sills. Once the basic shell was approved by management, it

was handed down to Plymouth Styling to define the outerskin.

Chrysler management also chose to give the platform to Dodge, initially as

an upscale competitor to Mercury's Cougar. Dodge had been offered its version of the Barracuda in 1964 or the option of having its own 117 in. wheel-

Matty Matsurra's sketch dated 7/26/68 for a full urethane front for the E-body. Unfortunately, the technology and budget was not *available to Chrysler to produce a true front urethane treatment.*

Rallye Instrument Cluster contained 150 mph speedometer, 8000 rpm tachometer, gauges for oil pressure, alternator, engine temperature and fuel. The last pod on right contained the clock. The Rallye Cluster was optional on the Barracuda, 'Cuda and base Challenger.

Standard instrument panel for the Challenger contained 120 mph speedometer and gauges for fuel, engine temperature and alternator. The far right-hand pod was blank unless the optional clock was ordered. The four switches at the left of the speedometer are for (top) headlamps and wiper and (bottom) headlamp dimmer and top lift (convertibles only).

The Challenger was the co-star with Barry Newman in the movie Vanishing Point. The Challengers used in the movie were powered by either 440 or 383 engines.

base sporty car. Dodge chose the latter and introduced the 1966 Charger, which was designed by a young stylist named Carl Cameron. Cameron, who had worked at Ford styling, was hired by studio chief Bill Brownlie in October 1962. While the decision to field the 1966 Charger had eventually proven profitable, Dodge management realized it had missed out on the explosive ponycar market. Jumping in this late may have been viewed as anti-climactic, but by sharing some costs with Plymouth, Dodge could spread around the dollars spent and be profitable while selling less units.

1970: All-New Barracuda and Challenger

The final designs of the 1970 Barracuda and Challengers would be different from each other, although to the casual observer, they looked similar. At the Plymouth studio, John Herlitz was primarily responsible for the Barracuda's outerskin. In an interview with Musclecar Review magazine, Herlitz recalled, "What we really wanted to do, or what I was after with the body side of the car, was to pull the rear quarters as high as possible and spank the roof

It didn't take long for factory drag teams like Sox and Martin to get the Hemi 'Cuda into the record books. Mr. Four-Speed was the Spring Nationals Pro Stock champ with a blistering 10.02/137.77.

down as low as possible and just get the very high hunched look in the rear quarters, allowing the front fenders to become the long, leading design element

that ran out past the power plant to give it a very dynamic thrust." Milt Antonick remembers the 1967 Barracuda SX contributed downstream to the 1970 Barracuda. "We tried to capture the organic form of the SX," Antonick said. "Especially the shape of the rear flank and the C-pillar."

At the Dodge studio, Chief Designer Bill Brownlie commissioned his staff to

work up the Dodge outerskin proposal. As the deadline approached, Brownlie contributed his own concept. Cameron, who supervised the Dart and Challenger platforms, remembers the skinning of the Challenger: "It was Brownlie's body side, which is the section through the door, that was selected." Brownlie chose to widen the body by flaring out the character line that echoes the profile of the upper beltline from the leading edge of the fender to the end of the quarter panel. The Challenger also had a more pronounced Coke bottle effect in

Carl Cameron's drafting of a design for the first Dodge Challenger was dated February 4/1967. Note the rear spoiler and the fish-type gills behind the front wheels that were echoed in the rear window design—all speaking of the car's Barracuda heritage. Carl Cameron

Gene Snow's Rambunctious Challenger cleaned house at the NHRA Dallas World Finals in October 1970, putting it to Ed McCulloch's 'Cuda 7.03/207.37 to win the Funny Car World Championships. It was also the first funny car to break the 200 mph mark.

The Shaker hood was offered with all 'Cuda engines in Argent Silver, matte black or body color.

the quarter, kicking up the rear deck and then rolling down to meet the tail-lamp panel.

Strangely, the two cars shared virtually no metal, nor did they have the same wheelbase. Originally, the Challenger's wheelbase was slated to be 111 in., the same as the Dart. Carl Cameron suggested to reduce it by 1 in. As Cameron remembers, "We were out in the 'stockade' where cars were viewed, and I suggested to Brownlie we make it longer so it would *look* different, it would *be* different and it wouldn't seem that we

were using the same chassis to build another body on it. Brownlie liked the idea and he got it changed. It wasn't really that costly. We had talks with the engineers about the complexity—and remember we used to build totally different floor pans just for dual exhausts. It wasn't that big of a deal then."

The Dodge version rode on a 110 in. wheelbase (the Barracuda was on 108 in.) but only picked up a fraction of interior rear seat room over the Barracuda. The Challenger was longer at 191.3 in. to the Barracuda's 186.7 in. and wider at 76.1 in. to the Barracuda's 74.7 in.

The Barracuda also had a character line, but it extended horizontally along the flanks, just above the front and rear wheel openings. Like the Challenger,

Next page
A 1970 'Cuda convertible with Rallye wheels.

the quarter panels kicked up to the high rear deck, however there was a distinctive curl in the sheetmetal beginning at the rear of the upper door above the handle, defining the top of the quarter panel and flattening out to the deck line. The wheel cutouts were also different. The Challenger's wheel openings were rounded at the top and the sheetmetal actually kicked in before forming the wheel lips. The Barracuda's wheel openings were flattened at the top with no flaring.

Designer Carl Cameron summed up the styling of the two cars: "To under-

What's Your Color?

As part of the eye-catching packages that Chrysler offered for its ponycars, the Barracuda and Challenger could be ordered in some of the wildest exterior colors ever painted on a car. For Plymouth's Rapid Transit System and Dodge's Scat Pack, audacious colors were essential for the youth market, and the Barracuda and Challenger were some of the grooviest on the street.

Barracuda
Blue Fire Metallic
Lime Green Metallic
Deep Burnt Orange Metallic
Sandpebble Beige

Challenger
Light Blue Metallic
Bright Blue Metallic
Dark Blue Metallic
Bright Red

Rallye Red
Burnt Tan Metallic
Black Velvet
Citron Mist Metallic
Ice Blue Metallic
Jamaica Blue Metallic
Ivy Green Metallic
Yellow Gold
Alpine White
TorRed
In Violet
Lemon Twist
Lime Light
Vitamin C

Light Green Metallic
Dark Green Metallic
Dark Burnt Orange
Beige
Dark Tan Metallic
White
Black
Cream
Light Gold Metallic
Plum Crazy
Sublime
Go-Mango
Hemi Orange
Banana

1970 Hemi engine with optional Shaker hood in matte black.

'Cuda interior featured high-back bucket seats and console. Note how the console is canted toward the driver.

Next page
The hockey stick stripe offered in 1970 with the engine callout in the stripe.

stand how significant the difference was between the Barracuda and the Challenger, consider the car as a loaf of bread, and remove a slice from the center. This slice is called a "body section." The Barracuda's body section is clean and simple in the sense that it came right off the beltline, went out to a peak and went right underneath with extreme

tumble under. The Challenger's body section shows it kicked out a little more than the Barracuda, came down at an angle and flared out to the character line and then back down and into the sill."

In the Plymouth studio, designer "Matty" Matsurra sketched a full urethane front end for the new E-body. "We wanted to get rid of the bright bumpers," Antonick said. "Unfortunately, we didn't have any development for urethane bumpers. I was told that GM's urethane bumper development was bigger than Chrysler's entire front

end development. We knew what was going on with urethane, but we didn't have the technology to do it. That was the frustrating part."

Although the budget wasn't available for Chrysler to develop urethane bumpers like GM (for example, the 1968 Pontiac GTO's front end was all urethane), the Elastomeric bumper option was

The taillamps were cut out of the blacked-out rear panel. The key lock was offset to the right-hand side of the panel because the design of the decklid did not permit a lock located on the centerline.

offered beginning in 1970. Borrowing technology from Oldsmobile's Rallye 350, high-density urethane foam was molded over unchromed bumpers and then painted body color. It had all the appearance of the GTO's Endura bumper at much less cost. And, unlike the GTO, the Elastomeric bumper could be ordered both front and rear.

Under the skin, both cars featured traditional Chrysler unit-body engineering and featured side guard beams in the doors to protect driver and passenger from side impacts. Up front, 0.90 in. torsion bars and independent lateral, non-

The 1970 'Cuda's body side had a character line that ran horizontally along the flank. The wheel openings were rounded on the Barracuda versus those of the Challenger. The Barracuda was completely unlike its predecessors in styling or execution. No longer restricted by the Valiant's platform, designer John Herlitz succeeded in putting together a long hood, short deck package that was fresh and dynamic.

parallel control arms with Oriflow shocks and a 0.94 in. antiroll bar were used; with the 426 and 440 engines, the bar diameter was increased to 0.92 in. Around back, the live rear axle was held in place by semi-elliptical leaf springs. A 0.75 in. antiroll bar was offered in some applications along with four leaves per spring. On big-block-equipped models, the right rear spring had five full leaves and two half leaves, while the left had six

The Rallye wheel was originally offered only in 14 in. diameter. It was restyled for 15 in. applications.

Front-end look at Ivy Green 1970 'Cuda shows deeply inset painted grille and wide air opening in lower valance. The fog lamps were standard in 1970.

Hurst Pistol Grip shifter was standard with A833 four-speed gearbox. Note the absence of a console.

Hood pins gave the Hemi 'Cuda a true race-car flair. To protect the paint, the wires were coated with plastic.

full leaves to handle the extra torque shock and reduce axle windup.

With the proviso that the E-body engine bay accommodate *every* engine displacement offered by Chrysler, a total of nine different engines were offered in the Challenger and Barracuda. With engine choices ranging from a 225 ci six-cylinder to the asphalt-melting 426

Hemi, both Challenger and Barracuda were able to compete in all stratas of the ponycar and musclecar market.

The Barracuda was completely unlike its predecessors in styling or execution. No longer constricted to the Valiant's

Previous page
The exhaust tips exited through the rear valance panel on the 'Cuda models.

The deeply inset grille was surrounded by Argent Silver, flanked by single headlamps. Note the parking lamp and turn signal also recessed into the grille.

As far as ponycar trunks went, the 'Cuda's was not better and no worse than the norm. The collapsible spare saved considerable room.

The Rally Instrument Cluster was an extra-cost item, as were the cloth and vinyl seats. The wood-grained steering wheel was standard. Several magazines complained of the seating and wheel position of the 1970 'Cuda. Note the accordion-style covering over the collapsible steering column.

platform, Plymouth designer John Herlitz had succeeded in putting together a long hood, short deck package that was fresh and dynamic. It was also heavier by about 200 lb., even though it was 6 in. shorter than the 1969. Part of this slight of hand had to do with the longer hood; the body had been moved forward 1 ft.

Car Life compared a 1969 340 Barracuda to a 1970 340 Barracuda by measur-ing front wheel centerline to the front bumper and from the front wheel to the top of the steering wheel rim. The 1969 measured 36 in. from wheel centerline to bumper and 41 in. from front wheel to steering wheel rim. The 1970 measured 41 and 48 in. respectively. As *Car Life* noted, "The driver has exactly one more foot of metal between him and the front bumper."

Up front, the Barracuda featured sin-gle headlamps and an Argent Silver-finished fascia with inset grille and park-ing lamps beneath the hatch-type hood. Beneath the bumper was a large air inlet and on 'Cuda models, round fog lamps. The taillamp panel was painted matte black, with rectangular taillamps. The luggage compartment keylock was off-set to the right side of the panel. Accord-ing to Antonick, the design of the deck-lid precluded locating the key lock in the traditional centerline location. The exhaust tips exited through the valance panels.

The Challenger used more chrome and brightwork for an upscale look. Dual headlamps were deeply recessed under the huge hood, and the grille was outlined with bright molding. "I did the grille very deep," said Cameron. "The Challenger was very flat-faced. There was not a very large physical air opening in that car. The lights were set back at an angle to funnel the air into that center opening." A large chrome bumper (Elas-tomeric was offered on both Challenger and Barracuda) separated the grille from

1970 Engine Options

Engine	225	318	340	383	383	383	426
Horsepower	145 @ 4000	230 @ 4400	275 @ 5000	290 @ 4400	330 @ 5000	335 @ 5200	425 @ 5000
Torque lb-ft	215 @ 2400	320 @ 2000	340 @ 3200	390 @ 2800	425 @ 3200	425 @ 3400	490 @ 4000
Compression ratio	8.4:1	8.8:1	10.5:1	8.7:1	9.5:1	10.5:1	10.25:1
Bore & stroke	3.40 x 4.125	3.91 x 3.31	4.04 x 3.31	4.25 x 3.38	4.25 x 3.38	4.250 x 3.38	4.250 x 3.750
Carburetion	Carter 1-bbl	Carter 2-bbl	Carter 4-bbl	Carter 2-bbl	Holley 4-bbl	Holly 4-bbl	2 Carter 4-bbl
Lifter type	Mechanical	Hydraulic	Hydraulic	Hydraulic	Hydraulic	Hydraulic	Hydraulic
Exhaust	Single	Single	Dual	Single	Dual	Dual	Dual

Engine	440	440
Horsepower	375 @ 4600	390 @ 4700
Torque lb-ft	480 @ 3200	490 @ 3200
Compression ratio	9.7:1	9.7:1
Bore & stroke	4.230 x 3.750	4.320 x 3.750
Carburetion	Carter 4-bbl	3 Holley 2-bbl
Lifter type	Hydraulic	Hydraulic
Exhaust	Dual	Dual

Transmissions

Standard	225/318/383 (2–bbl)	Three-speed manual		TorqueFlite automatic
	340/383	Heavy-duty three-speed manual	340/383	Four-speed manual
	440/440-6/426	TorqueFlite automatic		TorqueFlite automatic
Optional	225/318/383 (2–bbl)	Four-speed manual	440/440-6/426	Four-speed manual

The Dodge E-body went through a few names like Explorer, Conquest and Eliminator before the name Challenger was chosen. The R/T was the top performance model.

Under the wide E-body hood, Chrysler could install any engine in the product lineup from the 198 cube Slant Six to the behemoth 440 Six-Pack with plenty of room left for air con-ditioning compressors, power steering systems and power brake boosters.

Challenger featured wood trim on the door panels and instrument panel. Note the Challenger script in the upper right-hand instrument panel.

the lower valance panel with a large air inlet and round parking/signal lamps.

On standard Challengers, the flat hood swept up to the cowl and covered the wipers. The optional Power Bulge hood, designed by Rick Carrell and modeled by Ron Carson, featured twin scoops and concealed wipers. Both hoods had the name Dodge spelled out across the front.

Flush-fitting doorhandles and ventless side glass contributed to the smooth look of the Challenger's flanks. Around back, the deck latch panel was dominated by the large taillamps and a bright molding that capped the rear of the quarters and trailing edge of the decklid. The reverse lamp was in the center of the panel, a design that Cameron had trouble getting approved. "It had the name Dodge on it. That was the first time anyone had put a name on a back-up lamp. I had a heck of a time doing that because they didn't think it would meet state lighting standards."

The rear bumper echoed the front bar, and a radically rolled valance panel featured cutouts for the exhaust tips on optional V–8 engines with dual exhausts.

Next page
Taillamps extended nearly across the rear panel. Note the Dodge lettering across the reverse lamp and the exhausts under the notched valance panel.

The steeply raked windshield, rounded side glass and wide body accentuated the Challenger's low profile.

The Challenger was offered in two series: Challenger and Challenger R/T. Both series had three distinct models: hardtop, convertible and Special Edition (SE). The base Challenger was equipped with 225 six-cylinder or 318 V–8 engine, all-vinyl interior that featured buckets up front, three-spoke wood-grained

The Power Bulge hood could be ordered with the special black paint treatment and a wide body side decal.

A 1970 Dodge Challenger R/T convertible in Plum Crazy. Note the Shaker hood scoop and pop-open fuel filler cap: Dodge picked up on the 1967–1969 Barracuda's pop-open cap, first on the 1968 Charger and then the 1970 Challenger. Dodge placed the cap on the right side because, according to Dodge stylist Carl Cameron, ''studio head Bill Brownlie thought that if you ran out of gas, you wouldn't be on the traffic side of the car. You'd be on the shoulder.''

A pair of Plum Crazy Challenger R/T convertibles, both with Hemi engines. Because there were so many various combinations of hoods, stripes and options, it's unusual to find two Challenger R/Ts or 'Cudas exactly the same. Note the name Dodge spelled out on the Power Bulge hood.

steering wheel and standard instrumentation that included a large speedometer to the left of the steering column with four pods containing gauges for fuel, temperature and alternator to the right. The fourth pod contained the optional clock; otherwise it was left blank. Below and to the left of the speed-ometer were switches for lamps, wipers and accessories. Also to the left of the column was the heater control panel. Below the gauges to the right of the column was the optional radio. In the center of the instrument panel was the ashtray, and below that the cowl vent controls.

On Challenger R/T models, the 383 Magnum engine was standard, along with Power Bulge hood, heavy-duty drum brakes, variable speed wipers, F70x14 billboard tires and Rallye Instrument Cluster. The Rallye Cluster consisted of a wood-grained panel with four large pods containing a 150 mph speed-ometer with trip odometer, clock/tachometer, oil pressure gauge, temperature, alternator and fuel gauge.

A longitudinal tape stripe or bumblebee stripe around the tail was offered at no extra cost on the Challenger R/T. "I never did like the bumblebee thing that went across the back," recalled Cameron. "In fact, that was one of my most disappointing moments in styling. I had spent all these years and money going to Art Center to be a car designer and some yo-yos, some outsiders, were putting bumblebees on these cars."

When the SE package was ordered, a vinyl roof with "formal roof styling" and

The big 426 Hemi engine was a costly option
and also rare. Only five Hemi four-speed R/T
ragtops were built in 1970.

The front passenger area was spacious while the rear seat room was nonexistent. Note the wood-grain insert in the console and the Hurst Pistol Grip four-speed shifter.

The Challenger R/T badge appeared in the lower left-hand corner of the grille. Note the large air inlet in the lower valance to aid in airflow to the radiator. The Dodge logo appears in the center front of the hood.

a smaller backlight (styled by Mack King) was included. The SE roof was unique thanks to the seam pattern designed by Cameron. "The location of the seams on a standard vinyl roof run from front to rear," Cameron explained. "The SE seams ran from the windshield back beside the rear window to the base of the vinyl roof. This made the top appear lower in profile because you read the

The 1970 340 T/A Challenger interior was the same as the standard R/T interior. Note the Dodge logo on the wood-grained door panels.

The tape stripe for the 340 T/A ran from the front fender to just behind the door on the C-pillar. The T/A call out was part of the tape stripe. The displacement decal was below the stripe at the rear of the front fenders.

seams. It also looked wider from the rear. I thought I'd start an industry trend with that one." Also included were leather-faced seat upholstery and an overhead interior consolette with door ajar, fasten seat belt and low-fuel warning lamps.

The Barracuda was broken down into three series: Barracuda, Gran Coupe and 'Cuda in either hardtop or con-

Because of the fiberglass hood, T/A Challengers all had the radio antenna (when so-equipped) located on the right-hand quarter-panel. The ducktail spoiler was unique to T/A.

Next page
Panther Pink T/A Challenger was a rare color option in 1970. The raked look of the T/A was due to the G60x15 tires in the rear and the E60x15 tires up front.

vertible body styles. The Barracuda was the base series and was offered with the 225 six or the 318 V-8 and was basically outfitted like the base Challenger. The Gran Coupe was similar to the Challenger SE, with leather seat inserts (bolsters and seatbacks were vinyl) or lower-cost cloth insert and vinyl buckets. Also standard was an overhead consolette like the Challenger's. Unlike the Challenger SE, the vinyl roof was optional on the Gran Coupe. The standard engines were either the 225 six or the 318 V-8, although the 290 hp or 330 hp 383 cube engine could be ordered optionally.

The top performer was the 'Cuda series. The 'Cuda offered the 335 hp 383 engine as standard equipment with Power Bulge hood, hood pins and emblems that called out engine displacement on the outboard sides of the scoops. Unlike the R/T, the Rallye Instrument Cluster was optional on the 'Cuda.

Both the Challenger R/T and 'Cuda could be ordered with the Shaker hood scoop painted either body color, black crackle or Argent Silver. The Shaker scoop rose through a hole cut in the hood and was sealed with a gasket to reduce water leakage. When the engine would rev, the scoop would shake, which, according to Chrysler, "Puts on a song and dance right before everyone's eyes."

Offered on both the Challenger and Barracuda was a mind-numbing array of options and accessories. Buyers had a choice of two different road wheels, a multitude of stripes and decals, including the huge billboard stripe for the 'Cuda, or the thumping 440 engine with a trio of Holley two-barrel carburetors

The T/A's Six-Pack 340 engine was under-rated at 290 hp and could easily boil the hides. Quarter-mile performance was 13.99/100.0 mph.

The grille on the Challenger was deeply inset into the front. Note the Veed design of the front bumper. The alligator-type hood was different from the Barracuda's hatch-type hood.

that cranked out an underrated 390 hp and could flatten Hemis in the quarter-mile. Also offered was a bench seat, cruise control, power windows and racing mirrors. In all, there were literally hundreds of paint, stripe, wheel, hood and engine option combinations available. Rarely did two Challengers or Barracudas ever look the same.

The bumblebee stripe was a no-cost option on the Challenger R/T. Designer Carl Cameron detested it.

The Challenger interior was slightly more upscale than that of the Barracuda. Cloth and vinyl upholstery was available on order.

Dan Gurney, right, stands with his 1970 AAR
Trans-Am 'Cuda. With Gurney is Swede Savage, who drove the Number 42 'Cuda.

Swede Savage streaks by at Road America in   way to finishing second behind Mark Dono-
the Number 42 AAR Trans-Am 'Cuda on his   hue's Javelin.

Trans-Am E-Bodies

In the late 1960s, the SCCA Trans-Am series had attracted the interest of the racing press and enthusiasts as Detroit

The Dodge entry was driven by Sam Posey. Although Posey was an excellent driver, the Challenger never was a contender, even though it finished third in three out of eleven races. Team manager Ray Caldwell acid-dipped the Challenger's body, a common occurrence in Trans-am racing. It must have stayed in the vat a little too long, however, because at one race the roof collapsed on Posey's head. To solve the problem, Caldwell rented a Challenger, removed the roof, welded it to the race car and called the rental company to come get its car.

The AAR 'Cuda was offered in mid-model year to homologate the 340 'Cuda for Trans-Am racing. The strobe stripes increased in size by 4 percent running from rear to front. AAR stood for Dan Gurney's All American Racing, the team that campaigned the 'Cuda in the Trans-Am.

The AAR 'Cuda was powered by a special 340 engine that featured a trio of Holley carbs mounted on an aluminum intake manifold.

entered their ponycars in the fray. Ford and Chevrolet poured money and talent into winning the series and the prestige of advertising the victory. Early on, Ford had recognized the importance of winning the Trans-Am, and by 1967 had locked up its second championship.

To homologate the Camaro for the Trans-Am, Chevrolet released the Z/28 with its special 302 ci small-block and virtually swept the 1968 series. Ford countered in 1969 with the Boss 302, a special Mustang package that included the race-ready 302 ci engine, special suspension and distinctive graphics. The Penske-prepared Z/28s were too much for Ford, Pontiac and the AMC Javelin, walking away with the 1969 championship.

By 1970, the Trans-Am series had become so popular that manufacturers couldn't afford not to compete. "It really should be called a Trans-Am Manufacturer's Championship," noted Dan Gurney in 1969, "because it's got five, possibly six manufacturers fighting each other who are awfully interested in what it does for the sale of their automobiles."

For 1970, the players shuffled somewhat, with the Penske/Donahue team moving to American Motors, Bud Moore piloting the Mustang efforts, Jerry Titus entering a lone Firebird and Jim Hall of Chaparral fame handling the Camaros with Tony DeLorenzo and Jerry Thompson at the wheel. There were also two new factory-backed players—Barracuda and Challenger, built by Dan Gurney.

As primary contractor for Chrysler's Trans-Am racing efforts, Gurney's All American Racing received cars from

The AAR 'Cuda's Six-Barrel air cleaner mated to the underside of the fiberglass hood with a thick rubber seal.

Chrysler and, after stripping most of the stock components off, prepared the chassis for both the Challenger and 'Cuda. Gurney's California shop would reinforce all the factory body welds with additional heliarc welds, then install a complete roll cage tied to the floorpans. The rear axle received a pair of leading lines to reduce wheel hop. The lines went through the floorpan and anchored to the cross-member in the center of the pan. Once the Challengers were completed, they were shipped off to Ray Caldwell's Autodynamics in Massachusetts for final assembly and detail-

ing. Gurney handled the completion of the Barracudas.

To break the dominance of the Chevy small-block, Pete Hutchinson, manager of Chrysler's Trans-Am program, worked with the legendary Keith Black to build the engines for both teams. Black built a killer Chrysler small-block that put out in excess of 460 hp with a cross-drilled crank, four-bolt main bearings, forged rods good to 8500 rpm and a stacked gear oil pump. Out of that work also emerged a unique cast-iron Trans-Am cylinder head with larger ports. Black's 303.8 ci engine (the SCCA allowed destroked engines up to 350 cubes to be eligible for the Trans-Am engine ceiling of 305 ci) had the same bore of 4.04 in. as the stock 340, so the new heads could be fitted to the street motor.

Next page
A special fiberglass hood was built at Creative Industries, which also handled the other special components fitted to the AAR 'Cuda.

The two Chrysler teams consisted of Dan Gurney at the wheel of the number 48 Barracuda and teammate Swede Savage in number 42. The single car entry from the Massachusetts-based Caldwell team was piloted by second-year driver Sam Posey. Posey also happened to own Autodynamics and was Ray Caldwell's employer.

Like all the manufacturers, Chrysler was required to homologate its race cars by selling a certain quantity of special street versions. The SCCA had devel-

With its special suspension, large rear tires, big brakes and high-winding 340 engine, the AAR was an excellent road car.

oped a formula to determine how many cars had to be built for homologation based on the previous year's production: it worked out to 2,800 cars for the Barracuda and, since the Challenger had not been offered in 1969, a minimum number of 2,500 was stipulated for Dodge. To meet the homologation rules, Plymouth released the AAR 'Cuda and Dodge the Challenger 340 T/A.

The AAR 'Cuda and the 340 T/A Challenger were cosmetically different and mechanically identical. Working with Creative Industries, which also did the work on the Daytona and Superbird, Plymouth designer Milt Antonick designed the special hood scoop that was integrated into the fiberglass hood. Painted matte black, the hinged hood used locks up front. The tops of the fenders were also painted matte black to match. The hood and spoiler on the AAR was the same for both the street and race versions. The unique strobe stripes that ran along the upper beltline created

some problems for the Plymouth design team. "The strobe stripe was something of a challenge," Antonick recalled. "We asked ourselves, how in the world we were going to figure this out for 3M? One of the guys in design was a genius in math, and he calculated a 4 percent increase in block size from segment to segment."

The Challenger also had a hinged, matte black fiberglass hood, but the scoop was raised high above the hood surface. Scoops placed at the hood surface don't really "ram" air into the engine, because a boundary layer of

The Trans-Am AAR 'Cuda built and driven by Dan Gurney has been found and restored to its 1970 race specs. It is currently being raced in vintage competition and Trans-Am reunions. Dr. John Craft

dead air exists at the hood surface. The large "pursuit plane" scoop on the Challenger T/A was a dead ringer for the small dummy scoops placed on the 1969 'Cuda hood. A chin spoiler was also part of the T/A's exterior, as was a wide stripe that ran from the front fenders to just behind the door under the C-pillar. At mid-fender, inside the stripe was a break with the T/A logo. The 340 displacement decal appeared behind the front wheel opening. A ducktail spoiler was mounted on the rear deck.

Both the AAR 'Cuda and the 340 T/A Challenger shared the same drivetrains. SCCA rules dictated that the stock block and heads be used for competition, so under the fiberglass hood was a special edition of the venerable 340 engine. The cylinder block was stress-relieved with additional material added to the main-bearing area. The specially machined cylinder heads had slightly offset push-rods to allow for larger ports. The push-rods themselves were longer than stock 340 units and had special ends for rocker-arm adjusting screws. The rocker arms were offset with cast-iron adjusting screws, similar to those used in the 426 Hemi. The rocker shafts had additional lube-spreader grooves. While the mains were two-bolt, there was plenty of meat

to drill out for four-bolt modification. A double roller timing chain was standard, as was the aluminum intake manifold and a trio of two-barrel Holley carburetors with 1½ in. throttle bores for the center carb and 1¾ in. bores of the outers.

The 340 would exhale through cast-iron exhaust manifolds hooked to special, low-restriction two-pass mufflers located forward of the rear axle. The pipe would then loop out and curve around to exit through a chrome trumpet-style exhaust tip located under the body-side sill ahead of the rear wheel. The exhaust outlet tips, brackets, hangers and installation instructions were delivered in the car's trunk for dealer installation.

The Pete Hutchinson-Keith Black 340 engine was destroked to 303 cubes and generated a healthy 460 hp. While the 'Cuda and Challenger were strong enough for Trans-Am racing, the team did not have the development time to work out the rest of the bugs. Dr. John Craft

Either the A–833 four-speed manual gearbox or the Torque Flite automatic transmission was offered, hooked to a standard 8¾ in. rear axle with a 3.55:1 gearing. Standard brakes were power discs up front and 11 in. drums at the rear. Fitted to 15x7 in. wheels were Goodyear Polyglas GT tires, E60x15 at the front and G60x15 rear.

The Rallye suspension package was bolstered by front and rear antisway bars and heavy-duty shocks. The rear spring camber was increased to provide adequate ground clearance for the special side-outlet exhaust and the G60x15 rear tires.

The 340 T/A Challenger and the AAR 'Cuda were popular additions to the Plymouth and Dodge product line. Factory records indicate Dodge shipped 2,400 Challenger 340 T/As and Plymouth 2,724 AAR 'Cudas in the short time they were on the market. Unfortunately, Gurney, Savage and Posey didn't fare too well on the Trans-Am circuit; the best showing by the Barracuda was a

second-place finish by Swede Savage. Posey managed three thirds and one fourth. After the 1970 series, Chrysler, along with Chevrolet, Pontiac and series winner Ford chose to withdraw, leaving a rather hollow victory in the 1971 series to American Motors, the lone factory still racing in Trans-Am.

On the street, the new 'Cuda and Challenger R/T quickly earned a solid reputation for performance. The 340 equipped models were insurance beaters and still had the aggressive looks of their big-block brothers. As in years before, the high-winding power of the 340 and good handling of the E-body combined to make it an excellent road

Gurney's office in the AAR 'Cuda was Spartan. SCCA rules allowed the removal of the stock interior and dashboard. A full roll cage was tied to the chassis for driver safety and structural rigidity. Dr. John Craft

car. In many respects, the 340 'Cuda and Challenger R/T were the ultimate ponycars.

But the ponycar had also become a musclecar, and with the awesome 425 hp Hemi and the thunderous 390 hp 440 Six-Pack (the 'Cuda version was called the Six-Barrel), the straight-line performance of the musclecar overwhelmed the inherent agility of these ponycars. With the tremendous torque and extra weight of the big powerplants, the braking and handling of the 'Cuda and Challenger R/T were sacrificed for the lowest elapsed times. Most magazines that tested the 440 and 426 equipped versions complained about the poor braking and abject handling. But for per-

formance car buyers, these were the ultimate musclecars; considering sheer torque and neck-snapping acceleration, few cars could beat the Hemi 'Cuda or 440 Six-Pack Challenger.

With a new body and an impressive lineup of engines, Plymouth expected Barracuda sales to go ballistic, especially since the division was riding a winning streak that knocked perennial third-place holder Pontiac back into fourth position. The Barracuda's big boost in sales didn't materialize, selling just 22,877 units more than in 1969, truly a disappointment since 1969 was the third year of the styling cycle and the Barracuda had looked rather dated. The poor sales performance of Barracuda in 1970 was the first indication to Chrysler management that the life cycle of its sporty car might just be over.

For Dodge, the Challenger had been a rousing success. In its first year, 83,012 Challengers had left Dodge showrooms. At the same time, Charger sales fell from

Next page
In 1971, a group of Indiana Dodge dealers worked together to supply the Indianapolis Motor Speedway with a batch of 1971 Challengers for pace car and parade duties. Unfortunately, during the official pacing duties, one of the dealers, who had no experience in high-speed driving, crashed into a stand full of media. After the crash, it was several years before any car makers would supply pace cars for the 500 mile classic. This particular Challenger was one of the parade cars. William Holder

more than 89,000 in 1969 to just less than 50,000 in 1970. How many of those sales were lost to the Challenger has never been determined, however within the Charger's market niche, the redesigned Grand Prix and the new Monte Carlo certainly tightened up the competition for personal-luxury buyers. The Charger's styling was also three years old, and the Challenger's fresh new looks cer-

R/T Challenger with vinyl roof, optional luggage rack and Rallye wheels. The SE version had a padded, formal-style roof with a smaller rear window. The Challenger's tail lamps were restyled for 1971. The reverse lights were integrated into the taillamps and the Challenger badge appeared in the center of the lamp panel.

tainly drained away potential Charger sales.

1971: Last Year for High Horsepower

Like the rest of Detroit, Chrysler entered the 1971 model year knowing that the days of absolute horsepower were drawing rapidly to a close. The clamoring chorus of safety lobbyists, insurance companies and public officials was growing louder in its criticism of Detroit's musclecars. But, more urgent in the eyes of car makers, were the impending safety and emissions regulations that would require considerable engineering. Development money was being shifted from product planning to engineering as Chrysler and the other car makers struggled to meet Washington's demand for cleaner air and safer cars.

Consequently, 1971 was the end of the line for much of the performance options that buyers had become used to. The engine lineup was juggled, with the addition of a second six-cylinder engine and the deletion of the lower-performance 383 four-barrel engine. The 440 four-barrel engine was also eliminated from the lineup.

Now offered was the 198 cube six-cylinder, the 225 cube six, the 318 V-8, the 340 four-barrel, two- and four-barrel versions of the 383, the 440 +6 and the 426 Hemi. Compression ratios were lowered on all engines except the 225 six, the Hemi and the 440 +6, which climbed from 9.7:1 to 10.3:1. Chrysler also followed the industry trend of advertising net horsepower ratings as opposed to gross ratings. Net ratings are derived from dyno testing an engine encumbered with all belt-driven accessories and with exhausts in place, a more accurate accounting of the engine's true

LIMITED-TIME
RATE REDUCTION

RDA AYMAD11AA

BUSINESS REPLY MAIL
FIRST-CLASS MAIL   PERMIT NO. 350   HARLAN IA
POSTAGE WILL BE PAID BY ADDRESSEE

NO POSTAGE
NECESSARY
IF MAILED
IN THE
UNITED STATES

A 1971 R/T Challenger with upper beltline striping and hood decal. There were numerous stripe and decal combinations for Challengers and 'Cudas. Note the scoops on the quarter panel.

output when installed in a production vehicle.

Minor styling changes were made for both cars in 1971. The Barracuda received a facelift with quad headlamps and a recessed grille divided into six segments Veed at the center and nearly flush with the bumper line. Below the bumper was a large air inlet and a pair of round parking lamps; fog lamps were now optional for the 'Cuda. The 'Cuda also received a pair of four Argent Silver non-functional louvers in the front fenders. Gran Coupes and base Barracudas had Barracuda script at the top of

the doors at the cowl. Around back, the taillamp panel was also revised. Inside, the seat upholstery was restyled with cloth and vinyl; all-vinyl and leather surfaces were also offered. One addition to the lineup was a budget-priced Barracuda coupe with fixed rear windows.

The Challenger also received new front-end styling. Up front, the dual headlamps were retained. The grille was revised, split into two narrow bezels that extended across the entire opening between the headlamps. The air inlet and front valance panel were carried over. Around back the taillamps were restyled, reflecting the long, horizontal front-grille styling. The large exhaust cutouts remained in the rear valance.

Both the 'Cuda and the Challenger R/T came standard with the 300 hp 383 engine, rated at 250 hp net. Base transmission was a three-speed manual gear-

box with floor-mounted shifter mated to a 3.23:1 rear. The 340, 440 Six-Barrel (Six-Pack for Dodge) and the Hemi were optional. As before, the Dana 60 rear axle and heavier rear leaf springs were standard with the large engines.

Although it appeared in magazine advertisements, the 340 T/A Challenger wasn't offered in model year 1971 since Chrysler had pulled out of the Trans-Am series. Fortunately, much of the engine hardware offered in the 340 Six-Pack made its way into the Direct Connection parts book.

Chrysler also reduced its drag racing budget in 1971. Plymouth and Dodge so dominated the Pro Stock and Super Stock classes that, as *Super Stock and Drag Illustrated* noted, "they don't see any pressing need to improve their lead." With Ronnie Sox and Dick Landy still leading the charge, Chrysler prod-

SUPERCAR SHOWDOWN

Launching off the line, this 1971 Challenger R/T is set up right. The car has lifted up off the suspension, the tires have hooked up and it's all forward motion.

ucts continued to put everyone else on the trailer. Dodge also canceled the popular Performance Clinics put on by Dick Landy because of tight budgets.

The automotive press took Chrysler to task for the poor quality control on the Barracuda and Challenger. "We tended

not to stick with something if it wasn't working," Cameron reflected. "We'd design a new one instead of refine or modify it. There were some unusual things on that car. It had the biggest doors in the industry. We also at the time were using the largest molded door trim panel, and it tended to rattle. It also acted like a sound board and made any noise inside the door worse."

Perhaps one of the worst examples of quality control was the door-lock mechanism. The lock mechanism assembly

was so heavy that one could strike a locked door with their fist underneath the doorhandle and it would unlock the door. "It was heavy enough," Cameron recalled, "that you could actually move the sheetmetal in and out and the lock mechanism stayed there, which, in effect, unlocked the door."

Magazines like *Hot Rod* were also extremely critical of the lack of a decent suspension under the big-block versions. "You need only one journey through a quick corner," *Hot Rod*'s

Billboard stripes were the rage at Plymouth in 1971. These were not easy for assembly line workers to apply.

The 1971 Barracuda's front end was restyled with quad headlamps and split grille with three sections per side. The surround was either painted body color or Argent Silver. The hatch-type hood on the 'Cuda was retained by pins at the front. Note the lack of product identification on front of car. Only a tiny Plymouth plate is on the hood, partially obscured by the right-hand hood pin.

Steve Kelley noted, "to realize how much the monster-motor cars need the aft stabilizer." Available with the large engines was the Track Option with 9¾ in. Dana 60 rear gear and 3.54:1 ratio, dual-point distributor, seven-blade fan and limited-slip differential. "A Super Track Pack," noted *Hot Rod*, "is almost the same, but it has a 4.10 gear, plus power steering and front disc brakes."

Seat upholstery was restyled for 1971. Note optional cassette player/recorder on console.

With the top down, the 1971 'Cuda was one of the best looking convertibles of the pony-car breed. Unlike the Challenger, the 'Cuda exhaust tips exited through the rear valance panel. Four non-functional louvers painted Argent Silver were placed on the front fenders of the 1971 'Cudas.

Plymouth and Dodge painted their muscle-cars in wild shades of purple, green, yellow and orange. This 1971 340 'Cuda is shaded In Violet.

Tuff steering wheel was popular option in 1971. Wood-grained Rallye Instrument Cluster was one of the best looking and most functional gauge clusters offered.

While it was the last year for the high-horsepower torque monsters, it was also one of the best. For the enthusiast who savored the rocket-like acceleration and tire-melting power that only lots of cubes could provide, 1971 was the end of an exciting era of muscle. Automotive writer Terry Jackson remembers his 1971 440 +6 Challenger well: "When I floored the pedal and the TorqueFlite shifted from first to second, it would rip an

The Shaker hood scoop was again offered for all 'Cuda engines, with the displacement badge attached to the outboard sides of the Shaker. A Shaker decal in shatter-type print was affixed to the underside of the hood.

Previous page
The Go-Wing rear spoiler was an extra cost option and provided absolutely zero down force when driving around town. It did look good, though.

eight-track cartridge right out of the console-mounted player and slam it into the back seat!''

1972: No Longer a Musclecar

If high-performance enthusiasts had any doubts whether the end of the musclecar era was upon them, all they had to do was read the 1972 Challenger brochure: "The way things are today, maybe what you need is not the world's hottest car."

Factions within Chrysler management had already decided to pull the plug on the Barracuda and Challenger but chose to run the line as long as it could recover

some profit. Consequently, little was done to expand the product except to give the cars a facelift, discontinue the convertible models, maintain a short list of options and accessories, and axe most of the engines. The ponycar was no longer a musclecar as Dodge extolled the virtues of a Challenger without lots of cubes and tire-smoking torque: "Maybe what you need is a well-balanced, fully instrumented road machine. One with a highly individualized style, a well proportioned balance between acceleration, road holding, braking—you know the bit."

Amber Sherwood Green 1971 340 'Cuda with optional vinyl top and fog lamps.

Challenger was now divided into two series: Challenger and Challenger Rallye. The Challenger was powered by the 225 cube Slant Six rated at 100 hp. Two eights were offered, the 150 hp 318 two-barrel and the 340 four-barrel with 240 hp. The Rallye was identified by the Power Bulge hood and dummy air extractors in the front fenders with a decal package trailing from the extractors into the doors.

Up front, the Challenger received a large, rounded grille designed by Bob Ackerman, with a smaller inlet in the lower valance and round parking/turn lamps. The rear taillamp panel, styled by Jeff Godshall, consisted of two large lamps per side with the reverse lamps inside the inboard taillamp. The exhaust tips still exited under the lower valance on 340 models.

Little was done to the interior. The seating upholstery was revised and the Rallye Instrument Cluster was offered standard on the Rallye and optional on the base Challenger. The Rallye models also received heavy-duty suspension.

Next page
The 1972 Challenger's front end was styled by Bob Ackerman. The large grille opening was retained until the end of production in 1974. The 1972 Challenger received non-functional air extractors on the front fenders with a decal package that drifted back to the doors.

Over at Plymouth, the Barracuda had suffered the same fate. The same engine lineup was spread across the base Barracuda and 'Cuda series and, just like the Challenger, the options were divided between the two series. The Barracuda's

115

The 340 four-barrel engine was now the largest engine in the Challenger and 'Cuda lineup. Note the location of the air-conditioning compressor.

facelift consisted of a handsome new Argent Silver grille recessed into the front and flanked by single headlamps. The rear lamp panel housed round taillamps (two per side) with the reverse lamps contained within the inboard lamps.

Both Barracuda and Challenger had been overshadowed by the Duster and Demon, and both of the compacts could be outfitted with most of the same performance options. The compact coupes were cheaper to buy and insure than the ponycars, and became extremely popular with young buyers. In fact, the 340 Duster outsold the 'Cuda almost two to

one in 1972, a factor that helped to grease the skids to the Barracuda's demise.

1973: Sales Rebound

There was little change cosmetically in 1973 save for new bumpers with large, thickly padded bumper guards. The area surrounding the Barracuda's grille was now painted body color and the Challenger received a bright grille. The base

Inside, the interiors were little changed. The twin-spoke steering wheel was redone, as was the seat upholstery.

Before he switched to Challengers, Don Carlton campaigned this 'Cuda funny car named Motown Missile.

Next page
Classic lines of Challenger were retained right up through 1974. The vinyl top was optional. The taillamp panel was updated, with a matte black field and twin oval taillamps and Dodge nameplate in the center. The Challenger name in script appeared on the quarter-panels.

Challenger series was retained, although the Rallye was now an option. For Plymouth, the base Barracuda and 'Cuda models remained separate series.

Under the skin there were a number of refinements. For openers, the 225 Slant Six was dropped, leaving only the 150 hp 318 and 240 hp 340 V-8 engines. Other improvements included an electronic ignition system. Both engines received induction-hardened exhaust valve seats for use with unleaded fuel.

Interiors were only slightly revised, however the seats were reworked for more comfort. Still optional were front and rear antisway bars, power front disc brakes, 70 series tires and road wheels.

Even though the performance options and high-powered engines were long gone, sales for the Barracuda and Challenger rebounded, although not as strongly as the competition.

Model	1972 Sales	1973 Sales
Camaro	68,656	89,988
Mustang	125,405	134,867
Firebird	23,951	46,313
Javelin	26,184	30,902
Barracuda	18,450	22,213
Challenger	26,658	32,596

The 'Cuda and Barracuda received some new tape stripes and extra padding on the bumper guards for 1973 as Plymouth watched the Duster outsell the Barracuda. The Challenger was also in a holding pattern in 1973. It too, received stouter bumpers to meet federal requirements. The Rallye was no longer a separate model but now an option.

1974: The End of the Line

Chrysler's sporty car twins entered their last year of production with a few surprises. The 318 remained the base engine, however the 340 was dropped in favor of the stronger 360, which produced 245 net hp. The Rallye option and the 'Cuda continued to offer front and rear antisway bars and F7014 tires. On the Rallye Challenger, the Rallye Instrument Cluster with full instrumentation, three-speed wipers and heavy-duty shock absorbers were also standard.

Chrysler management chose to withdraw the Barracuda and Challenger from production in March 1974, as America staggered under the first Arab oil embargo. Final production for the Challenger totaled 16,437 units, while Plymouth built 6,745 Barracudas and 4,989 'Cudas.

The death knell sounded in March 1974. After producing just 6,745 Barracudas, 4,984 'Cudas and 16,437 Challengers, production was halted.

122

Barracuda and Challenger 1975

Rest in Peace

The 1974 Barracuda and Challenger models were the end of Chrysler's involvement in the ponycar market. "I thought that was a big mistake," Carl Cameron recalled. Sales for all ponycars were soft, but were showing an upward trend that would reach its apex at the end of the decade. "We got out of the only part of the market that grew," Cameron noted. "We abandoned that."

A significant part of the problem, in the opinion of former Chrysler employees, was that management was now heavily comprised of finance people that had little feel for the marketplace or the product. And, because the finance people now made significant decisions regarding product, the "car guys" who understood the marketplace no longer had the clout to push product through the system. Many also point to 1968, when Chrysler had a record year but chose not to invest the money in product development. "Our primary business was designing, building and selling cars," one former employee said. "The money wasn't put back into product. Instead it was used to diversify into other areas, some of which were losers that cost Chrysler dearly."

There was also internal controversy about product. Many inside Chrysler questioned the decision to make the Challenger longer and wider than the Barracuda. Sharing body shells would have saved the corporation a considerable amount of money that could have gone into product development. Others blamed management for refusing to

build a subcompact to compete with the Vega and Pinto as the demand for the small cars reached a crescendo during the first oil crisis. Losing big car sales and missing the subcompact market were two blows that sent Chrysler reeling.

The postmortems would come later, because in the spring of 1969, the Plymouth styling studio was working on the next generation Barracuda. At that time, Chrysler had a four-year lead time from design to production and no one expected the cars to be canceled, so it was business as usual in the styling studios.

Two designs slowly evolved, one created by Matty Matsurra and influenced by Don Hood's clays, the other by

the team of John Herlitz and John Sampson. Both worked separately, however they studied each other's concepts and shared ideas. "We struggled to define the fourth-generation design," recalled Milt Antonick. "We wanted the car to look more fluid and yet retain that muscular and aggressive look." The teams thought it was important to preserve the ramps found in the curve of the E-body's front fender and rear quarters and to be sensitive to retaining some product image.

The fluid look was advanced by Herlitz and Sampson, while Matsurra's clays carried a more muscular theme. "We started somewhat conservatively with

Shunsuke "Matty" Matsurra's clay dated 4/14/69 shows a wedge-shaped rear and mid-engine look. "We were uncomfortable with the extractors," recalled Milt Antonick. "It lacked character."

variations on the Barracuda theme," recalled Antonick. "We then deliberately pushed the design theme as far toward a fluid muscular look as possible." The team discovered that doing so only exaggerated the theme.

After numerous cycles of sketches and clays, the teams narrowed it down from four designs to two. The two cars were viewed by Plymouth and Dodge design studios. "I saw them," remembered Carl Cameron, "and they were beautiful. Matty Matsurra did some beautiful body sides. They were neat and I liked them."

The final car was actually a blend of both Matsurra's and the Herlitz and Sampson design. "Because we had two models," Antonick said, "we retained a variation of the Barracuda's fender forms on one clay and tried to enhance it on the other." The vestiges of the 1970-1974 'Cuda fender forms were still intact, while the fluid look was evident in the rolling quarter panels and hood.

In the fall of 1969, the prototype car was taken to a consumer survey group in Cincinnati. The results were not good. "That wild body went to Cincinnati of all places and it was a disaster," said Antonick. "I came back from Cincinnati and realized it was all over, they didn't want musclecars anymore. It was the saddest day of my career at Chrysler." As if an omen, the Cincinnati car fell off a forklift during transport and was damaged.

Although the studio was instructed to prepare some "nose jobs" for the current car to extend its life beyond 1974, it was obvious to many in Plymouth Design that the Barracuda and the Challenger were doomed.

Although Henry Ford dismissed history as "bunk," the fact remains that the ponycar enjoyed a tremendous resurgence in the 1970s and early 1980s. That Dodge and Plymouth were not there to share in the bounty remains as one of many glaring failures of Chrysler product planners and management, who envisioned a world of Volares, Aspens, Omnis and Horizons. "Unfortunately," observed Carl Cameron, "back then we always went after the basic transportation guy and left the specialty market and the high-level, high-profit items to General Motors and Ford."

Would the radically redesigned Barracuda and Challenger have shared in the revitalized ponycar market? The clays indicate an aggressive, exciting car that would have dated the Firebird and Camaro and rendered them obsolete. "I think our cars would have been competitive," observed Cameron. "We would have kept the marketshare that we had."

But would the hypothetical success of the Chrysler ponycars have kept the corporation from the brink of bankruptcy? While that question will never be answered, enough factors exist to make a valid argument that Chrysler would have been healthier. GM's decision to retain its ponycars proved to be profitable. At its lowest point in 1973, the Pontiac Firebird sold just 29,951 units of all models. By 1979, sales had exploded to more than 211,000. The Camaro tallied 89,988 units in 1973, and climbed to 282,571 in 1979. Ford's 1973 Mustang, in the last year of its cycle, sold 134,867 copies. Even the star-crossed Mustang II sold 385,993 units in 1974, and the new 1979 Mustang registered 369,936 sales in 1979.

The decline and fall of Chrysler Corporation reads like a classic tale of managerial incompetence in an under-

Don Hood's "Vestige" clay, so named because it echoed vestiges of the 1970-1974 Barracuda, especially the strong ramps on the front fenders and rear quarters. This clay preserved many of the lines used in the E-body to preserve the product's image.

The "Cincinnati" car. This clay shows how the inner door skins, side glass, windshield and sill could have been carried over from the E-body. This proposal was the result of marrying the Matsurra and Sampson-Herlitz designs. The full-length rear spoiler was retained. To attain the roofline as shown, designers planned to recline the rear seat passengers. Also by moving the rear header back, it allowed more headroom for the rear-seat passengers. Obviously, a quarter window would have been necessary, and the rest of the proposal would have been revised to meet bumper standards and other requirements.

capitalized, aging company that erred at a time when mistakes in the marketplace were deadly. "Chrysler doesn't do anything first," noted *Car and Driver*. "Instead, it carefully watches what everybody else in Detroit is doing and when it sees an area of abnormal market activity it leaps exactly onto that spot. Because it always leaps late—which is inevitable if it doesn't begin to prepare its entry into the market until some else already has one—it tries to make up for being late by jumping onto said spot harder than everybody else." In the mid- to late-1970s, Chrysler failed to hit the right spots, and the only salvation was a government bailout.

Those were the worst of times. For the men and women who designed and engineered the Barracuda and the Challenger, they can point to a happier era when the Chrysler ponycars were the equal of Ford's Mustang and GM's Camaro and Firebird. They can point to the enviable reputation the 'Cuda and the Challenger had on the street and on the drag strip. For those involved in the Barracuda and Challenger, they were truly the best of times.

The post Cincinnati nose job. This photo was taken October 30, 1969, a few weeks after the Cincinnati massacre. Since the same body was to be retained, Don Hood's aerodynamic look was grafted onto a production 'Cuda. The scoops would have been functional.

Several different ideas were tried, including recessed and hidden headlamps, stripes and decals. Note the chin spoiler and the overall resemblance to the Ford King Cobra Torino. It was also turned down.

Production Figures

All production figures quoted here represent Chrysler statistics on the number of cars shipped during a given year, which may differ from the number of cars actually built during that year.

1964 Barracuda
Hardtop coupe six-cylinder	2,647
Hardtop coupe eight-cylinder	20,796
Total	23,443

1965 Barracuda
Hardtop coupe six-cylinder	18,567
Hardtop coupe eight-cylinder	41,601
Total	60,168

1966 Barracuda
Hardtop coupe six-cylinder	10,645
Hardtop coupe eight-cylinder	25,536
Total	36,181

1968 Barracuda
383 automatic	516
383 four speed	754
Formula S Package	1,120
Total	46,018

*Base cars includes all base six-cylinder and V-8 models.

1969 Barracuda
Hardtop six-cylinder	4,203
Hardtop eight-cylinder	7,548
Convertible six-cylinder	300
Convertible eight-cylinder	973
Sport coupe six-cylinder	2,163
Sport coupe eight-cylinder	12,205
Total	27,392

1969 Barracuda Performance Engine Production
Model	Hardtop	Convertible	Fastback
340 'Cuda automatic	30	0	166
340 'Cuda four speed	68	0	402
383 automatic	45	10	272
383 four speed	53	7	331
383 'Cuda automatic	61	0	248
383 'Cuda four speed	33	0	130
440 'Cuda	NA	NA	NA
Formula S 340 Package	325	83	1,431
Formula S 383 Package	98	17	603

1967 Barracuda

Convertible	4,228
Coupe	28,196
Fastback	30,110
Total	62,534

1967 Barracuda Performance Engine Production

273 4bbl automatic	6,847
273 4bbl four speed	1,036
273 Formula S Package	5,352
383 Formula S Package	1,840
383 automatic	748
383 four speed	1,036

1968 Barracuda

Base cars	39,698*
340 automatic	2,461
340 four speed	1,469

1970 Barracuda Performance Engine Production

Barracuda	Coupe	Hardtop
383 4bbl automatic	2,540	132
383 4bbl four speed	1,905	68
440 4bbl automatic	618	28
440 4bbl four speed	334	6
440 6bbl automatic	852	12
440 6bbl four speed	902	17
426 automatic	368	9
426 four speed	284	5

1970 Challenger

Challenger	
Deputy Hardtop	1,265
Hardtop	38,091
Convertible	2,543
SE	5,858
Challenger R/T	
Hardtop	13,668
Convertible	955
SE	3,741

1970 Barracuda

Barracuda		Hardtop	7,109
Coupe	520	Convertible	532
Hardtop	17,196	'Cuda	
Convertible	1,164	Hardtop	16,710
Barracuda Gran Coupe		Convertible	548

1970 Barracuda Performance Engine Production

Barracuda	Coupe	Hardtop	Convertible
383 4bbl automatic	1	464	36
383 4bbl four speed	2	602	17
Barracuda Gran Coupe	Coupe	Convertible	
383 4bbl automatic	732	63	
383 4bbl four speed	341	17	
'Cuda	Hardtop	Convertible	
340 4bbl automatic	3,392	155	
340 4bbl four speed	3,492	88	
340 T/A automatic	1,604	0	

1971 Barracuda

Barracuda	
Coupe	592
Hardtop	6,508
Convertible	722
Barracuda Gran Coupe	
Hardtop	1,331
'Cuda	
Hardtop	5,383
Convertible	292

1971 Barracuda Performance Engine Production

Barracuda	Coupe	Hardtop	Convertible
383 4bbl automatic	4	91	9
383 4bbl four speed	5	78	10
383 4bbl three speed	2	7	0
Barracuda Gran Coupe	Hardtop	Convertible	
383 4bbl automatic	79	0	
383 4bbl four speed	16	17	
383 4bbl three speed	3	0	
'Cuda	Hardtop	Convertible	
340 4bbl automatic	2,008	102	
340 4bbl four speed	1,141	30	
340 three speed	154	0	
383 4bbl automatic	1,168	87	
383 4bbl four speed	501	33	
383 4bbl three speed	67	16	
440 6bbl automatic	129	12	
440 6bbl four speed	108	5	
426 automatic	48	5	
426 four speed	59	2	

1970 Challenger Performance Engine Production

Challenger	Hardtop	Convertible
Deputy		
383 4bbl automatic	3	0
383 4bbl four speed	3	0
Challenger		
383 4bbl automatic	952	84
383 4bbl four speed	457	31
Challenger SE		
383 4bbl automatic	644	0
383 4bbl four speed	158	0
Challenger R/T		
440 4bbl automatic	1,886	129
440 4bbl four speed	916	34
440 6bbl automatic	793	38
440 6bbl four speed	847	61
426 automatic	150	4
426 four speed	137	5
Challenger RT/SE	Total	
383 4bbl automatic	2,076	
383 4bbl four speed	400	
440 4bbl automatic	733	
440 4bbl four speed	142	
440 6bbl automatic	161	
440 6bbl four speed	135	
426 automatic	37	
426 four speed	22	

1971 Challenger

Challenger		Convertible	1,793
Coupe	2,053	Challenger R/T	
Hardtop	17,914	Total	3,907

1971 Challenger Performance Engine Production

Challenger	Coupe	Hardtop	Convertible
383 4bbl automatic	9	412	126
383 4bbl four speed	8	107	41
Challenger R/T			
383 4bbl automatic	1,985		
383 4bbl four speed	465		
440 6bbl automatic	121		
440 6bbl four speed	129		
426 automatic	12		
426 four speed	59		

1972 Barracuda

Barracuda	10,622
'Cuda	7,828

1972 Challenger

Challenger	18,535
Challenger Rallye	8,128

1973 Barracuda

Hardtop coupe eight-cylinder	9,976
Hardtop coupe 'Cuda eight-cylinder	9,305
Total	19,281

1973 Challenger

Total	27,930

1974 Barracuda

Hardtop coupe eight-cylinder	6,745
Hardtop coupe 'Cuda eight-cylinder	4,989
Total	11,734

1974 Challenger

Total	11,354

Index